THE COMMERCIAL POLICY OF ENGLAND
TOWARD THE AMERICAN COLONIES

"How often have the English commercial restrictions on the American colonies been treated as if they were instances of extreme and exceptional tyranny, while a more extended knowledge would show that they were simply the expression of ideas about the relation of dependencies to the mother country which then almost universally prevailed."

William Edward Hartpole Lecky, *Forum,* xiv, p. 721.

"To answer this question we must know not merely what those laws enacted, but to what state of colonial trade they originally and successively applied. For instance, what, from time to time, by development of agricultural or other industries, between 1640 and 1774, had the colonists to sell, and what, as they increased in wealth, did they wish to purchase?"

Mellen Chamberlain, Winsor, *Narrative and Critical History of America*, vi, p. 63.

"Nous sommes portés à croire que les privilégiés les ont usurpés par la force ou par la ruse, au lieu que le plus souvent ils n'ont fait que les accepter et les subir."

Fustel de Coulanges, *Histoire des Institutions Politiques*, i, p. 136.

"It is supposed for instance that the revolt of our own American colonies was provoked by the selfish treatment of the mother-country, which shackled their trade without rendering them any benefit in return for these restraints. This is far from being true. Between England and the American colonies there was a real interchange of services. England gave defence in return for trade privileges."

J. R. Seeley, *Expansion of England*, p. 65.

STUDIES IN HISTORY, ECONOMICS AND PUBLIC LAWS

EDITED BY

THE UNIVERSITY FACULTY OF POLITICAL SCIENCE

OF COLUMBIA COLLEGE

Volume III]   [Number 2

THE COMMERCIAL POLICY OF ENGLAND

TOWARD THE

AMERICAN COLONIES

BY

GEORGE LOUIS BEER, A. M.

NEW YORK

PETER SMITH

1948

PHOTOLITHOGRAPHED BY
THE MURRAY PRINTING COMPANY
WAKEFIELD, MASSACHUSETTS

TABLE OF CONTENTS.

[5

CHAPTER I. ENGLAND'S COLONIAL AND SHIPPING POLICY BEFORE THE RESTORATION.

§ 1. *General Introduction.* In literature the most permanent results are obtained by describing accurately some phase of the psychological and social life of man. If, however, an author starts out to solve some intricate problem, to illustrate some crying evil, he must inevitably fail in the purely literary quality of his production. The love and labor should be devoted to the description; the *morale* will follow as its inevitable concomitant. Corresponding to the writer who uses literature merely as a means, is the doctrinaire in science. If an historian starts out with a preconceived idea, he may, by fitting the facts to his theory, produce a most fascinating and symmetrical book. But we can place no reliance on the result obtained. Much labor will have been wasted to illustrate a theory of the author, or to defend an inherited prejudice. In science, as in literature, to produce the highest and truest results we must not set to work to prove any theory. In the one case we lose in scientific, in the other, in literary value. For the historian the only true method is to critically examine and to impartially describe the facts, to place them in logical order, and then, if he deems it necessary, to draw the inevitable conclusion. Induction, not deduction, is the historical method.

Unfortunately this spirit has rarely been characteristic of American historians, when treating of the relations of England and her colonies. They start with the idea that England consciously pursued an egotistic and tyrannical policy.

By making the facts conform to this preconception, they have produced books that are notably unjust to England.[1]

In view of the prevalent philosophy of evolution, we should before condemning the policy of any age look not at its absolute, but at its relative, efficiency. No institution can be condemned from the historical standpoint, if it is really in advance of that which preceded. From the modern democratic standpoint the absolute monarchy must be condemned as a form of state organization. But as regards liberty and the development of nationality, the absolute monarchy was certainly a step in advance of feudal anarchy. Nor even, if on the surface a retrogression appears, should we be hasty in our condemnations. Rome by too great centralization finally reached a condition where further progress was impossible. The Teutons then destroyed the Roman civilization, and introduced one much more primitive. But, on the other hand, they brought into prominence the spirit of individualism:[2] and it is this, combined with the Roman principle of unity, which has rendered the modern state possible.

From the days of Charles II. to those of Adam Smith, the policy of England was based upon the principles of the mercantile system, itself a marked advance on the balance of bargain theory which preceded. Toward her colonies England acted on this principle, and its necessary consequence was that colonial trade should be confined to the home market. For Child's opinion, "That all Colonies or Plantations do endamage their Mother-Kingdoms, whereof the Trades of such Plantations are not confined by severe Laws,

---

[1] *Cf.* H. L. Osgood's "England and the Colonies," *Political Science Quarterly*, ii, p. 440.

[2] Attilio Brunialti, *Lo Stato Moderno*, p. 25; Burgess, *Political Science and Comparative Constitutional Law*, i, p. 36.

and good execution of those Laws, to the Mother-Kingdom"[1] was the dominant one in England.

In the light of the modern ideas of *laissez-faire* and free trade this policy is condemned; but to the men of those days it was as true as is the theory of evolution or of diminishing returns to us. It was a policy of unconscious ignorance, not of conscious malice. History teaches that ignorance disguised in the garments of truth has, quite as often as malice, caused the adoption of erroneous policies.

The desire moreover to make the colonies contribute to the benefit of England was a most natural and reasonable one. The English people had lost many lives and had expended vast sums in colonization, both directly and indirectly. Prof. Seeley maintains that the ultimate cause of the vast and frequent wars of England from William III. to George IV., was the rivalry of England and France in India and in America. He says: "But in our wars with Louis XIV. before and in our wars with the French Revolution afterwards, it will be found on examination that much more than might be supposed, the real bone of contention between England and France is the New World."[2]   From this point of view it appears that England incurred a vast debt by protecting and maintaining her colonies, and why should she not expect them to yield some benefits in return?

And when we compare England's policy with that of other countries, we can see how much more liberal England was. Thus Leroy-Beaulieu says, "*l'Angleterre se montra même sur certains points d'un libéralisme inusité à l'époque dont nous parlons.*"[3]   And even Lecky, whose strictures on England's colonial policy are very severe, says: "It is a

[1] Child, *New Discourse of Trade* (2nd ed., London, 1694), p. 79; *cf.* Huskisson, *Speech on the Navigation Laws* (London, 1826), p. 9.

[2] Seeley, *Expansion of England*, p. 32.

[3] *Histoire de la Colonisation chez les peuples modernes*, p. 119.

gross and flagrant misrepresentation to describe the commercial policy of England as exceptionally tyrannical."[1]

All institutions and policies are the result of a process of growth, and the colonial policy of England from the days of Charles II. is no exception to this rule. The two germs from which it sprang, can be found far back in English history; first, protection to shipping, second, the desire to make the colonies inure to the benefit of the home country. The first duty of the writer will be to trace these lines of development till they became united in the acts of Charles II.

§ 2. *Navigation Acts before 1603.* The reign of Richard II. was characterized by great social and economic unrest. The outward manifestations of this were the success of the teachings of Wyclif, and the uprising of Tyler and his followers. This reign "marks the beginnings of the policy which was embodied in the Corn Laws, of the Navigation Laws, of the deliberate manipulation of commerce with the object of procuring bullion."[2] Thus, at the time when the son of a Hull merchant,[3] Michael de la Pole, was made Chancellor and Earl of Suffolk, the first navigation acts were passed. To increase the diminished navy of England all merchandise was to be exported and imported in "ships of the King's liegeance."[4] In the following year the conditions prescribed in this law were relaxed, so that when sufficient or suitable English ships could not be obtained at the place where the merchant dwelt, foreign ones might be employed.[5] To prevent exorbitant charges, eight years later it was

---

[1] *History of England*, iii, p. 327. See Adam Smith's *Wealth of Nations*, ii, pp. 155, 156.

[2] W. Cunningham, *The Growth of English Industry and Commerce*, Early and Middle Ages, p. 338.

[3] Campbell, *Lives of the Lord Chancellors* (London, 1856), i, p. 248.

[4] 5 Richard II., *Stat.* i, c. 3.   [5] 6 Richard II., c. 8.

enacted that merchants should freight in English ships, provided a reasonable recompense were demanded.[1]   The reference is probably to the mediæval doctrine of *justum pretium.*[2]
During the disorders of foreign and domestic wars in the
next century, these laws most naturally were not enforced.

In 1440, the commons petitioned the king, Henry VI.,
that "thenceforward no Italian or other merchant of the
countries beyond the straits of Morocco, should sell in this
realm any other merchandize than of the countries beyond
the straits, on pain of forfeiture thereof."[3]   Although rejected, this petition contained the germs of the later policy
of confining ships to carrying the products of the country
where they belonged.[4]

Edward IV. took up the policy again, and in the third
year of his reign it was enacted that no stranger or alien
should export wool, and "that no person inhabiting within
this realm of England, other than merchants strangers"
. . . . "shall freight nor charge within this realm of
England or Wales, any ship or other vessel of any alien or
stranger, with any merchandises to be carried out of the
said realm of England or Wales, nor shall bring into the
same,"[5] if he could find sufficient English vessels.   This
statute was, however, enacted for only a very short period.[6]

The first of the Tudors, the economical Henry VII.,[7] continued the policy of Richard and of Edward.   In 1485 a
statute was passed providing that no wines of Guienne or
Gascony should be imported except by Englishmen, Irish-

---

[1] 14 Richard II., c. 6, "les possessours des ditz niefs preignent resonablement
pur le frette dicelles."

[2] *Cf.* for the theory, Ashley, *English Economic History and Theory*, i, p. 132.

[3] Reeves, *A History of the Law of Shipping and Navigation*, p. 12; Hume,
History of England, ii, p. 434.

[4] Reeves, p. 13; Macpherson, *Annals of Commerce*, ii, p. 444.

[5] 3 Edward IV., c. 1.   [6] It was for three years.   [7] 1 Henry VII., c. 8.

men or Welshmen, and in their ships. A few years later the
provision was extended to woad imported from Toulouse,[1]
and it was provided that in all cases Englishmen should give
the preference to native ships, employing foreign ones only
when the number of English ships was not adequate.[2]
Though Sir Francis Bacon was apparently unacquainted
with the acts of Richard II., his observations concerning
Henry's policy are most judicious. He writes, "bowing the
ancient policy of this estate from consideration of plenty to
consideration of power: for that almost all the ancient statutes
invite (by all means) merchants strangers to bring in all
sorts of commodities; having for end cheapness, and not
looking to the point of state concerning the naval power."[3]

Henry VII. was, however, accustomed to permit by license
the violation of these laws. In 1492 he granted a license to
John Kendal, to import fifty tuns of Gascon wine in ships
belonging to England, or to its friends and allies.[4] Later
we find a license to Julian, ambassador of the King of
Naples, permitting him to import one hundred tuns of woad,
"*in aliqua navi extranea.*"[5]

Henry VIII. frequently sold licenses for the importation
of wine and woad contrary to the provisions of his father's
statutes. In 1509 we find a license to import one hundred
tuns of wine from Gascony and Aquitaine.[6] The number of
licenses was increased so rapidly as to render the law of
Henry VII. nugatory.[7] On account of this, in the seventh

---

[1] 4 Henry VII., c. 10, § i.

[2] 4 Henry VII., c. 10, § ii.   Proprietor, master, and mariners must be English.

[3] *Works* of Bacon [ed. Spedding, Ellis, Heath], xi, p. 145.

[4] Rymer, xii, p. 487, "*in navibus de obedientia nostra aut aliquorum Amicorum & Confoederatorum.*"   [5] Rymer, xii, p. 558; *cf.* also xii, p. 566.

[6] Brewer, *Letters and Papers of Henry VIII.*, i, p. 54; *cf.* also p. 63.

[7] Schanz, *Englische Handelspolitik*, i, 370; i, 370 n. gives a list, compiled from Reeves, of all the licenses granted; *cf.* Reeves, p. 16.

year of the reign, an act was passed repealing all these licenses.[1] Notwithstanding this, in 1518 Henry granted to his French Secretary a license to import four hundred tuns of Gascon wine in any foreign vessel.[2]

After Wolsey's fall the laws of Henry VII. were re-enacted,[3] but later it was made legal for the King to repeal these laws and to reënact them by proclamation.[4] To prevent the demand of exorbitant prices, the price of wine was fixed.[5] Rates for carrying these commodities were to be determined, but in time of war they might be raised.[6] These laws did not answer their purpose, for the navy declined[7] and the prices demanded for wine and woad were excessive.[8] On account of this Edward VI. repealed the laws of Henry VII.,[9] and Elizabeth those of both Henry VII. and Richard II.[10] Later she reënacted the law of Henry VII.[11] and provided that the coast trade be reserved to English ships.[12]

Thus we see that from the days of Richard II. England legislated for the protection of her own shipping. The succession of statutes is nearly continuous, and at no time do we find that the act of Richard II. was lost sight of by English legislators.

§ 3. *The Fundamental Cause for Colonization in the Six-*

---

[1] 7 Henry VIII., c. 2.

[2] Rymer, xiii, p. 620 in "*aliquibus Navibus Franciæ, Hispaniæ, Britanniæ, Portugaliæ, Flandriæ, Holandiæ, Brabandiæ, aut Zellandiæ, seu alicujus alterius Nationis.*"   [3] 23 Henry VIII., c. 7.

[4] Henry VIII., c. 10. In 1539 Henry granted a license to his surgeon to import 600 tuns of Gascon wine, Rymer, xiv, p. 645.

[5] 23 Henry VIII., c. 7; 28 Henry VIII., c. 14.   [6] 32 Henry VIII., c. 14.

[7] 5 and 6 Edward VI., c. 18, § ii; Cunningham, *Growth of English Industry and Commerce*, i, p. 435 n; ii, pp. 20, 21.

[8] 5 and 6 Edward VI., c. 18, § ii. Coke, *On Trade* (London, 1671), p. 51.

[9] 5 and 6 Edward VI., c. 18.   [10] 1 Elizabeth, c. 13.

[11] 5 Elizabeth, c. 5, § xi. D'Ewes, *Journals* (London, 1682), p. 88.

[12] 5 Elizabeth, c. 5, § viii.

teenth Century. Greece founded her colonies because the small size of the country allowed no room for expansion. In Rome, political and military reasons led to colonization.[1] But Europe in the sixteenth century did not suffer from overpopulation, nor did the same social structure exist as had prevailed in Roman times. When Columbus and Vasco da Gama opened new worlds to Europe, *gain* was the ultimate motive that led to the colonization of these regions.[2] Gold was the loadstar of Cortes, De Soto, Pizarro, and of other heroes of that age.[3] In England we can perceive the same influence, though to a less degree. What Sir Walter Raleigh sought in Guiana in 1595, was gold.[4] In the letters patent to Adrian Gilbert, "golde and silver oare, pearles, jewels, and precious stones" are mentioned as the commodities he is seeking.[5]

In the patent which Queen Elizabeth granted to Sir Humphrey Gilbert it is stated that he was to pay the Queen one-fifth part of all gold and silver mined.[6] In the rent that Vir-

---

[1] Blanqui, *History of Political Economy* [translated by Leonard], pp. 229, 230; Adam Smith, *Wealth of Nations*, ii, pp. 135–137; M'Culloch, *Dictionary of Commerce and Navigation*, p. 346.

[2] J. R. Seeley, p. 40: "When the floodgates are thrown open, there is no stream ready to flow, for in Europe at that time there was no superfluous population seeking an outlet, only individual adventurers ready to go in search of gold. Columbus can make no progress but by proving to the sovereigns that the territory he discovers will yield revenue to *them*."

[3] Christopher Columbus "*nos enseño este nuevo mundo tan colmado de oro*," Oviedo, *Historia de las Indias* (Salamanca, 1547), p. 58; *cf.* also pp. 53–58.

[4] Sir Walter Raleigh, *The Discovery of Guiana*, (Hakluyt Society, Vol. 3), p. 3; *cf.* Stebbing, *Sir Walter Ralegh*, p. 116.

[5] Hakluyt, *Voyages* (London, 1600), iii, p. 96. *Cf.* also the patent, "*de Potestatibus ad Terras Incognitas Investigandum*," where "*Aurum et Argentum in Massa, Lapides preciosas*" are especially mentioned, Rymer, xiii, p. 37, and Hazard, i, pp. 12, 13; compare also the Maryland charter of 1632, Preston, *Documents Illustrative of American History*, 1606–1863, p. 65.

[6] Hakluyt, iii, p. 135.

ginia, Massachusetts and the other colonies were to pay the King we can see the same desire for gold. In the first Virginia charter the company was required to pay one-fifth of all the gold and silver, and one-fifteenth of all the copper mined.[1] Likewise in the charter to Massachusetts Bay of 1629 the same rent, one-fifth part of gold and silver ore, is demanded.[2] That gold was what the first colonists to Virginia sought is well known. Captain John Smith writes, " but the worst was our guilded refiners with their golden promises made all men their slaues in hope of recompences; there was no talke, no hope, no worke, but dig gold, wash gold, refine gold, loade gold, such a bruit of gold that one mad fellow desired to be buried in the sands, least they should by there art make gold of his bones."[3] Likewise we read in Anderson, " after the Virginia Company had, at several different times, raised by subscriptions from their adventurers a capital of no less than two hundred thousand pounds, still, in vain *hoping for gold and silver mines*, and other very rich productions, many of them at length became weary of the charge."[4]

While at the outset England had the same object in aiding colonization as Spain, fortunately she soon saw the error in her policy. While Spain exploited her colonies for the advantage of the royal treasury, officials and priests, England administered her colonies for the advantage of the mercantile

---

[1] Preston, p. 7. *Cf.* also the grant of Nova Scotia to Sir W. Alexander, Hazard, i, pp. 135, 136; Maryland Charter of 1632, Preston, p. 66.

[2] Preston, pp. 40, 41, 42, 45, 46.

[3] *Travels of Captaine John Smith* (Richmond, 1819, from London, 1629), i, p. 169. Compare also Beverley, *History of Virginia*, i, pp. 17, 18; Beverley, *Relation Historique de la Virginie* (Amsterdam, 1718), pp. 25, 26; Sainsbury, *Calendar*, 1661–1668, p. 25, John Giffard makes proposals about mines of gold and silver, and precious stones in New England.

[4] Anderson, *Origin of Commerce*, ii, p. 415; *cf.* M'Culloch, *Dictionary of Commerce*, p. 348.

classes.[1] The common sense of the English people contributed to this result. But more than this was that fact of importance that England found in her colonies no Potosi, and
had to relinquish *nolens volens* the dream of vast treasures
from mines.

Theoretically, the title to new lands in the sixteenth century was derived from prior discovery. The English title to
North America thus rests on the discoveries of the Cabots.[2]
Therefore it will be of interest and value to examine how
trade was regulated in the patent[3] granted in 1496[4] to John
Cabot and his sons. Cabot was required always to return to
the port of Bristol, and the reason was that the king might
receive one-fifth part of the profits of each voyage.[5] The
patent does not, as is usually assumed, lay down the principle that the colonial trade should be limited to the home
market. For it merely provides that in return for freedom
from customs on all goods imported from the newly discovered lands, and in return for a monopoly of the trade
thither, the king was to receive one-fifth of the net profit.
To ensure the payment of this, the ships had to return to
Bristol.

Dated March 19th, 1501, is a patent to Richard Warde,

[1] Roscher, *Kolonien, Kolonialpolitik und Auswanderung,* p. 243.

[2] Hazard, i, p. 603; Sainsbury, *Calendar,* 1661–1668, p. 177.

[3] Hakluyt, iii, 4, 5; Hazard, i, pp. 9, 10.

[4] 1496, not 1495 as given by Hakluyt. *Cf.* Biddle's *Cabot,* p. 72.

[5] *Ita tamen, ut ex omnibus fructibus, proficuis, emolumentis, commodis, lucris,
& obuentionibus ex huiusmodi nauigatione prouenientibus, praefatus Johannes,
& filii ac haeredes, & eorum deputati, teneantur et sint obligati nobis pro omni
viagio suo, toties quoties ad portum nostrum Bristolliæ applicuerint (ad quem
omnino applicare teneantur & sint astricti) deductis omnibus sumptibus & im-
pensis necessariis per eosdem factis, quintam partem capitalis lucri facti, siue in
mercibus, siue in pecuniis persoluere.* Hakluyt, iii, p. 4; Hazard, i, p. 10. The
translation of the critical passage, as given by Hakluyt, iii, p. 5, is, "At the
which port they shall be bound and holden onely to arriue."

Thomas Ashehurst and John Thomas of Bristol, and to John and Francis Fernandus and John Gunsolus of Portugal.[1] In this patent there are various commercial regulations. A monopoly of trade to the newly-discovered land is granted for ten years.[2] And in return for the *"grandia custus et onera"* of the adventure, the patentees were to receive certain exemptions from customs duties. Thus annually for four years they might import into England one cargo of commodities duty-free.[3] But more important are certain sentences from which we can infer that the trade of the patentees was to be confined to the mother country.[4] The next year, another charter was granted to three of the former associates, Thomas Ashehurst, Francis Fernandus, John Gunsolus, and to one Hugh Eliot.[5] This patent is called *"de Potestatibus ad Terras Incognitas Investigandum."* The monopoly is here prolonged to forty years, and various other minor changes were introduced. Again the same sentences occur, from which the intention of confining the trade to England is apparent.[6] The evident meaning and purpose of both these patents are that the trade arising in consequence of the grants should be

---

[1] Biddle's *Cabot*, Appendix, p. 312.   [2] *Ibid*, p. 314.   [3] *Ibid.*, p. 315.

[4] Biddle, pp. 314, 315. *"Et ulterius ex abundanti gratia nostra concessimus,"* etc.

[5] Rymer, xiii. p. 37; Hazard, i, p. 11.

[6] *"Et ulterius ex habundanti Gratia nostra Concessimus & per Præsentes Concedimus pro Nobis & Hæredibus nostris, quantum in nobis est, præfatis Hugoni, Thomæ, Johanni, & Francisco, & eorum cuilibet, Hæredibus & Assignatis suis, quod ipsi & eorum quilibet Mercandisas, Mercimonia, Aurum et Argentum in Massa, Lapides preciosas, & alia Bona quæcumque de Crescentia Patriarum, Insularum & Locorum prædictorum, per ipsos sic recuperandorum & Inveniendorum, tam in dictis Navibus et Batellis quam aliis quibuscumque Navibus Exteris a dictis Patriis, Insulis, Terus firmis, & Locis in hoc regnum nostrum Angliæ ad quemcumque Portum seu alium Locum ejusdem adducere & cariare . . . "* Rymer, xiii, p. 38, and Hazard, i, pp. 12, 13. *Cf.* also *"percipiant de Bonis & Mercimoniis, a dictis Insulis, Terris firmis, & Patriis in hoc Regnum Angliæ Adducendis,"* Rymer, xiii, p. 39.

confined to England, so that the king may gain an increased revenue from the customs. Moreover, in regard to the payment of these the patents are very explicit.

All through his long years in prison it was the dream of Raleigh to revisit Guiana, and to bring home to England vast treasures.[1] In 1616 an opportunity was afforded him by King James[2] and the commission then granted states that Raleigh shall return to England and there pay one-fifth part of all gold and silver to the King.[3]

Thus at one time in England, as well as in Spain, desire for the precious metals was the chief cause which led men to undertake the work of colonization. The transition from the policy of gaining riches by mining and by seizing the precious metals from ignorant savages, to one of commercial monopoly is most interesting and natural. The sovereigns of England, in order to gain their share of the gold or profit, forced the navigators and discoverers to return to the port whence they had started, or to some other port of England. If now the object of the voyage were so changed as to be wholly commercial, and a permanent settlement were established in the newly discovered territory, we should then have the full development of one principle of the colonial system, *viz.*, the confining of the colonial trade to the home market.

[1] S. R. Gardiner, *Prince Charles and the Spanish Marriage*, i, pp. 41-49, gives an excellent account of Raleigh; *cf.* Stebbing's *Ralegh*.

[2] *De commissione speciali directa Waltero Rawley Militi concernente Voiagium Guianianum*, Rymer, xvi, p. 790. This patent, although it chronologically belongs to the next era, logically belongs to this. For Raleigh's exploits fall in line with those of the Elizabethan sailors, rather than with those of the colonists of the Stuart era.

[3] "And from thence to Returne, Import, Convey and Bringe into this our Kingdome or any other our Dominions, such Gould, Silver, Bullion, or anie other Wares Merchandizes or Commodities whatsoever as they shall thinke most fitte and convenient" and then "Payinge and Answeringe unto Us our Heires and Successors the full fifte Parte, in fives Partes to be devyded, of all such Gould and Silver and Bullion, or Oare of Goulde and Silver and Pearle or Precious Stone, as shall be imported." Rymer, xvi, p. 790.

It may be well to notice here a marvelous essay by Sir Francis Bacon, entitled "*Of Plantations.*" In it he speaks against this desire for gold, saying, "for the hope of mines is very uncertain, and useth to make the planters lazy in other things;"[1] and he adds, let there be "not only freedom from customs, but freedom to carry their commodities where they may make their best of them, except there be some special cause of caution."[2]

§ 4. *Colonial and Shipping Policy of James I. and Charles I.* The patents which were discussed in the last section, were not so much charters for founding colonies, as permissions to discover and bring under the dominion of England new lands. With the accession of James a new era opens in colonial history, the epoch of actual settlement.

It should always be remembered that the reigns of the first two Stuarts covered a most troubled period in European history. The continent suffered from the devastations of The Thirty Years' war, and in this struggle both James and Charles were interested on account of their relation to the Elector Palatine. In England itself developed the conflict between democratic Puritanism and *jure divino* Anglicanism. When viewed from this standpoint, it does not appear strange that in this period no definite colonial policy was evolved.

In the first Virginia charter (1606), James granted to the London Company a temporary monopoly of trade. It was allowed to impose a tax on anything "trafficked, bought or sold" by persons "of any Realms, or Dominions under our Obedience" or by "Strangers, and not Subjects under our Obeysance." In the first case the tax was to be two and

---

[1] Bacon, *Works*, xii, p. 196. "*Verum fodinis ne confidas nimium, præsertim a principio. Fodinæ enim fallaces sunt et sumptuosæ, et spe pulchrâ lactantes, colonos reddunt circa alia socordes.*"

[2] *Ibid*, p. 197.

one-half per cent., in the latter five per cent.[1] After twenty-one years the income arising from this tax must be paid to the king.[2] In 1622, the King issued a proclamation forbidding any one but adventurers and planters in New England to trade with the Indians, or to cut trees in the woods.[3] In the charter of 1629 to Massachusetts Bay, certain exemptions from customs and privileges in the payment of them were granted for limited periods.[4] In 1642, the Long Parliament showed its friendly spirit to the New England Puritans by exempting from customs all goods exported to New England, or imported thence into England.[5]

These various provisions show a desire to foster colonies in their infancy, but in them we can find no germs of the restrictive policy which England was in later times to adopt. Other acts, however, show the connection between the Stuart policy and that of both their predecessors and successors. The evident meaning of the grant to Lord Baltimore in 1632 is, that all merchandise should be sent from Maryland to England, and could then be reëxported to foreign countries.[6]

---

[1] Preston, p. 9.   [2] *Ibid.*, p. 10.

[3] Rymer, xvii, pp. 416, 417, "*De Proclamatione prohibente Anticipationem Commercii ad Partes Novæ Angliæ in America.*"   [4] Preston, p. 53.

[5] Hazard, i, pp. 494, 495; Winthrop, *History of New England*, [ed. Savage], ii, p. 98; Chalmers, *Political Annals*, pp. 174, 175; Bishop, *History of Manufactures*, i, p. 303.

[6] We grant license " to import, unlade, by themselves or their servants, factors or assigns, all merchandises and goods whatsoever, that shall arise of the fruits and commodities of the said province, either by sea or land, into any of the ports of us, our heirs and successors, in our Kingdoms of England or Ireland, or otherwise to dispose of the said goods, in the said ports, and if need be, within one year next after unlading the same, to lade the same merchandise and goods again into the same or other ships, and export the same into any other countries either of our dominion or foreign (being in amity with us, heirs and successors). Provided always that they pay such customs, impositions, subsidics, and duties, for the same, to us, our heirs and successors, as the rest of our subjects of our Kingdom of England, for the time being shall be bound to pay." Preston, pp. 72, 73; Scharf *Maryland*, i, p. 57.

An order of the Privy Council, dated October 24th, 1621, directs that all tobacco and all other commodities from Virginia should be landed in England, whence, after paying the customs, they might be shipped to foreign countries.[1] In the instructions to Sir William Berkeley in 1641 we can see the same idea. He is to be very careful that no vessel depart thence before bond be taken to carry the commodities to his majesty's dominions, so that his majesty "may not be defrauded of what is justly due for customs on the goods."[2]

Thus we can see that in the first half of the seventeenth century the policy of confining colonial trade to the home market existed in the mind of the government. Let us now inquire whether there are any traces during these reigns of the policy of protecting English shipping. It was seen above how Elizabeth reënacted the laws of Henry VII.[3] In 1622 James I. ordered a committee to take into consideration " how our Laws do now stand in force for the prohibiting of Merchandize to be ymported in Forrain Bottoms."[4] In 1624 a proclamation ordered that no tobacco should be imported in foreign bottoms, on pain of confiscation of both the tobacco and the vessel.[5] On July 7th, 1629, Charles issued a proclamation "that noe Wynes whatsoever shall be hereafter imported into this our Realm, or the Domynions thereof in any For-

---

[1] Sainsbury, *Calendar of State Papers*, 1574–1660, p. 26.

[2] Chalmers, *Political Annals*, p. 120; pp. 132, 133; Sainsbury, *Calendar of State Papers*, 1574–1660, p. 321.

[3] 5 Elizabeth, c. 5, § xi; D'Ewes, p. 88.   [4] Rymer, xvii, p. 414.

[5] Rymer, xvii, pp. 623, 624. "And whereas Wee are informed that some Traders in Tobacco do use to ymporte Tobacco in forrayne Bottoms, We straightly chardge and command that noe Person Whatsoever, either Stranger denizen or naturall borne Subjecte, presume to ymport any Tobacco whatsoever in any forraine Bottom at any time hereafter, upon Pain of Confiscation not only of the said Tobacco but also of the Ship or Vessell wherein the same is so ymported and upon the other Paynes and Penalties aforesaid."

aigne Shipp, Hoye, or other Vessel whatsoever, contrary to the Laws and Statutes of this our Realme."[1] A few months later, Charles ordered the laws of Richard II. and of Henry VII. and VIII. to be put in execution, "which Lawes of later yeares have been much neglected to the greate prejudice of the Navigation of our Kingdom."[2] About a year after the execution of Laud, January 23rd, 1646, Parliament enacted that all customs on merchandise (except the excise) shall be remitted on goods sent to Virginia, Bermudas, Barbadoes, and other places of America. If, however, the plantations sent away goods in foreign bottoms, they should not be exempted from the customs.[3]

So during the reigns of Charles and his father we find here and there references to the policy of confining the colonial trade to the home country. Likewise we can see that the policy of protection to English shipping was not dormant, while in connection with it the idea was also appearing that English and colonial ships should have the monopoly of the trade between the mother country and the colonies.

In this connection it may be well to notice the policy of the Stuarts toward that most important commodity, tobacco. Here again we shall find the germs of many subsequent acts. To Sir John Hawkins is attributed the introduction of tobacco into England in 1565.[4] The stimulant rapidly grew in favor, and in a few years became almost a necessary of life. It is said that in London in 1614 there were seven thousand shops selling tobacco.[5] That the use of tobacco was already very

---

[1] Rymer, xix, p. 95.   [2] *Ibid.*, p. 130.   *Cf.* the other regulations in this document.

[3] Hazard, i, pp. 634, 635; Holmes, *Annals of America*, i, pp. 282, 283; Reeves, pp. 32–34.

[4] *10th Census of U. S., Agricultural Statistics*, "A Succinct Account of Tobacco in Virginia," by Brock, p. 213; Dowell, *A History of Taxation ana Taxes*, iv, p. 266; *Arber*, English Reprints, x, p. 85.

[5] *Autobiography of Lord Herbert of Cherbury* [ed. Lee], p. 210 n.

common can be seen from the frequent allusions of contemporary writers. Although not referred to by Shakespeare, Beaumont and Fletcher,[1] Dekker[2] and Jonson[3] mention it quite frequently. Besides its use as a stimulant, tobacco was in those days used as a medicine. Lord Herbert, of Cherbury, the historian of Henry VIII., says that he was forced to take tobacco as a remedy "against certain rheums and catarrhs."[4]

In many countries of Europe opposition was made on moral and religious grounds to such extensive use of tobacco.[5] In Massachusetts we find the opposition expressed in various public acts. In 1633 a law ordered the constable to bring all idlers, such as tobacco-takers, before the magistrate.[6]

[1] *Knight of the Burning Pestle*, Act i, Sc. iii, "Fie, this stinking tobacco kills me! would there were none in England!—Now, I pray, gentlemen, what good does this stinking tobacco do you? Nothing, I warrant you: make chimneys o' your faces!" *Ibid*, Act v, Sc. iii, "I thank you all, gentlemen, for your patience and countenance to Ralph, a poor fatherless child; and if I might see you at my house, it should go hard but I would have a bottle of wine and a pipe of tobacco for you."   [2] *Gull's Hornbook* (Bristol, 1812), pp. 17, 18.

[3] *Every Man in His Humour*, Act iii, Sc. ii, "Ods me, I marl what pleasure or felicity they have in taking this roguish tobacco. It's good for nothing but to choke a man, and fill him full of smoke and embers: there were four died out of one house last week with taking of it, and two more the bell went for yesternight; one of them, they say, will never scape it: he voided a bushel of soot yesterday, upward and downward. By the stocks, an there were no wiser men than I, I'd have it present whipping, man or woman, that should but deal with a tobacco-pipe: why, it will stifle them all in the end, as many as use it; it's little better than ratsbane or rosaker." *Cf.* also *Bartholomew Fair*, Act ii, Sc. i. For many other references, compare *Arber's English Reprints*, x, pp. 81–94, 113–120.

[4] *Autobiography* [ed. Lee], p. 210.   [5] Dowell, iv, p. 269.

[6] *Colonial Laws of Massachusetts*, 1672–1686, p. 66, and 1660–1672, p. 158; *Colonial Records of Massachusetts*, i, p. 109. In 1632 it was enacted that no person take tobacco publicly, and for every offence a penalty was fixed. *Ibid.*, p. 101; *cf.* also i, pp. 126, 136, 180, 204, 241, 242, 385, 388, 403. In 1646, the general court enacted that no person should take any tobacco "in any comon ground, or feild inclosed, or yardes" upon a fine of 2 sh., provided nevertheless, that any man might in his journey, when five miles distant from any house, take tobacco, "so that thereby hee sets not ye woods on fire to ye damage of any man." *Ibid*, ii, p. 151; *cf.* iii, p. 68.

James I. was a most vigorous opponent of the use of tobacco, except as a medicine, and in support of his views he published the celebrated " Counter-blaste."[1]

In 1604 James, in addition to the former duty of two pence, imposed a custom of six shillings eight pence on every pound of tobacco imported.[2] Tobacco was also planted to quite an extent in England.[3] James endeavored to stop the culture in England, since tobacco tended " to a generall and new Corruption both of Mens Bodies and Manners[4]:" in 1619 and 1620 by proclamation he ordered that no one should plant tobacco in England.[5]

About this time the Virginia Company had a dispute with James concerning tobacco. By letters patent of May 23rd, 1609, the king had granted to it an exemption from all taxes except five per cent. Notwithstanding this, the farmers of the customs demanded one shilling per pound on Virginia tobacco. At this time Virginia tobacco was worth only three to four shillings.[6] The company objected to paying this, and the attorney-general decided in their favor.[7] When, however, the king, as mentioned above, prohibited the growth of tobacco in England, the company in return agreed to pay the additional duty.[8]

Soon after the company had granted this increased duty, the king issued a proclamation restraining the quantity of to-

---

[1] *A Counter-Blaste to Tobacco*, London, 1604, printed in Arber's *English Reprints*, x, pp. 95–112.

[2] Rymer, xvi, pp. 601, 602. Tobacco is " Excessivelie taken by a number of ryotous and disordered Persons of meane and base Condition, whoe, contrarie to the use which Persons of good Callinge and Qualitye make thereof, doe spend most of there tyme in that idle Vanitie, to the evill example and corrupting of others." For a brief account of the history of tobacco, *vide* Hubert Hall, *The Customs-Revenue of England*, i, pp. 175, 176, 178, 180.

[3] Rymer, xvii, p. 190.   [4] *Ibid.*, p. 233.   [5] *Ibid.*

[6] Stith, *History of Virginia* (London, 1753), p. 168.

[7] *Ibid.*, p. 169.   [8] *Ibid.*, p. 170.

bacco to be imported from the Virginia and Somers Islands to 55,000 pounds, and at the same time he granted a monopoly to certain persons.[1]   Since the Somers Islands were dependent upon the tobacco trade, Virginia allowed them to send the full amount to England.   The Virginia company, however, procured store-houses and appointed factors at Flushing and Middleburg, and then sent all their tobacco to Holland.[2] The king was incensed, and Virginia was ordered to send its entire product to England.[3]

Soon after this incident (in 1622) Lord Treasurer Middlesex tried to make the company "consent to their own oppression and squeeze out of them a greater Profit and Revenue to his Majesty," by making a contract with them.[4] The most important articles of the contract[5] were:

I. The Virginia Company and the Somers Islands Company were to have the monopoly of importing tobacco into England and Ireland.

II. No tobacco was to be planted in England.

III. The company was to pay to the King "the clear Proceed of a full third Part of all Tobacco" imported.

IV. For two years the company had to import from 40,-000 to 60,000 pounds of Spanish tobacco.[6]   The last provision was obviously introduced to promote the success of the negotiations concerning the Spanish marriage.

The next year this contract was dissolved,[7] and from that time on we have attempts to establish a royal monopoly. James, in 1624, at a time of great resentment against Spain, acting on a petition of the Commons,[8] prohibited the importation of any tobacco except from Virginia or the Somers

---

[1] Stith, pp. 198, 199.   [2] *Ibid.*, p. 200.   [3] *Ibia.*, p. 203.

[4] *Ibid.*, p. 244.   [5] *Ibid.*, p. 247.   [6] *Ibid.*, p. 248.

[7] E. D. Neill, *History of the Virginia Company of London*, p. 394.

[8] Sainsbury, *Calendar*, 1574–1660, p. 63; *cf.* p. 69.

Isles.[1]   The intention was also to make the tobacco trade a royal monopoly.[2]

Charles I. was not so frantically opposed to the use of tobacco as his father had been.   Soon after his accession, at the beginning of 1626, he entrusted to a commission the duty of seizing all illegally imported tobacco.[3]   This commission could also at its discretion import Spanish tobacco, though the amount thus brought in should not exceed 50,-000 pounds a year.[4]   These commissioners were also " to buy and contract for all such Tobacco, as shall growe, be made, or vented in our Plantations or Colonyes of Virginia."[5]   Charles frequently forbade the cultivation of tobacco in England.[6]   A proclamation of 1627 required that all tobacco should be imported directly to London.[7]   Later it had to be landed at a particular wharf.[8]   Then foreign tobacco was wholly excluded, and plantation tobacco was admitted only under license and on the condition that it be sold to the king's commissioners.[9]   Licenses were likewise required for selling tobacco at retail,[10] and a commission was appointed to see that this was carried out.[11]   On the 19th of June, 1634, Charles appointed a commission, of which Sir Dudley Digges was a member.[12]   This body was given the right of preëmption on all tobacco grown on the plantations.[13]

[1] Rymer, xvii, p. 622; xviii, p. 19.   [2] Ibid., pp. 668, 669.   [3] Ibid., p. 852.

[4] Ibid., xviii, p. 833; cf. p. 849, p. 886; also Sainsbury, Calendar, 1584–1660, p. 83.

[5] Rymer, xviii, p. 833.   [6] Ibid., p. 19; p. 849; p. 886; p. 921.

[7] Ibid., p. 849; xix, p. 235; Sainsbury, Calendar, 1584–1660, p. 84.

[8] Rymer, xix, p. 553.   [9] Ibid., xviii, p. 921.

[10] Ibid., xix, p. 474; p. 522.   [11] Ibid., xx, p. 16.   [12] Ibid., xix, p. 560.

[13] Ibid. Brock, p. 224, gives the following table of exports of tobacco from Virginia :

1619	20,000 lbs.	1628	500,c00 lbs.
1620	40,000 lbs.	1639	1,500,000 lbs.
1621	50,000 lbs.	1640	1,300,000 lbs.
1622	60,000 lbs.	1641	1,300,000 lbs.

Cf. Stith, p. 246.

Purely economic motives did not lie at the basis of the policy of James and Charles towards tobacco. During the reigns of these two monarchs commercial policy was subservient to political and fiscal needs. The quarrels with their parliaments and their consequent need of money, drove the Stuarts to the policy of monopoly. James prohibited the growth of tobacco in England, principally because he thought that the consumption of tobacco produced in Northern climates was injurious to the health.[1] The idea of giving the colonies a monopoly was secondary, and only later did it come into great prominence. The prohibition of the importation of Spanish tobacco arose more from resentment against Spain than from a desire to protect the Virginia product.

§ 5. *The Acts of 1650 and 1651.* The commercial highway of the nations during the middle ages was the Mediterranean, and it is to this fact that the prosperity of the Italian and Rhenish cities can be attributed. In the fifteenth century a great change occurred. In 1453 the Turks captured Constantinople and a large part of the Eastern trade was cut off. Forty years later came the discoveries of Columbus and Vasco da Gama and the consequent opening of new trade routes. Commercial supremacy was then transferred from the states of the Mediterranean to those of the Atlantic coast. The sixteenth century saw the rise of Spain, Portugal, France, England, and the United Provinces, as well as the decline of the German and Italian cities.

The United Provinces were populated in the main by burghers possessing the special aptitude of that class for com-

---

[1] Rymer, xvii, p. 621, the tobacco of England and Wales is "utterly unfyt in respect of the clymate to cherishe the same for any Medicinall Use, which is the only Good to be approved in yt." For fuller information, *cf.* the index of Sainsbury's *Calendar*, 1584–1660.

merce.[1] The Dutch quickly adapted themselves to the change of circumstances. England in the time of Elizabeth was not a naval power; not until the seventeenth century did she begin to make rapid strides forward in naval affairs.[2] At the middle of the seventeenth century the superiority of the Dutch over the English in commerce and navigation was as great as, at the beginning of the nineteenth, was that of England over the continental countries in manufacturing.[3] As the English saw the benefits arising from the Dutch carrying trade, they began to feel intense jealousy. This phase of the rivalry between the two nations found an indirect expression in the controversial writings of Selden and Grotius. The feeling of rancor[4] among the English remained dormant through the reigns of James and Charles, but during the Commonwealth it burst forth in legislative acts.

The Dutch carried on a very prosperous trade with the

---

[1] Cf. Pringsheim, Beiträge zur Wirtschaftlichen Entwickelungsgeschichte der Vereinigten Niederlande im 17. und 18. Jahrhundert, in Schmoller's Forschungen, x, iii, pp. 1–3.

[2] Sheffield, Commerce of the American States (Lond., 1784), p. 136, says that the tonnage of England was in 1581, 72,450 tons; in 1660, 95,266 tons; in 1675, 190,533 tons; in 1700, 273,693 tons; in 1750, 609,798 tons; in 1774, 798,864 tons.

[3] Edinburgh Review, li, pp. 419–427; Macpherson, ii, p. 442.

[4] To Sir Walter Raleigh is attributed a dissertation, whose purpose it was to abstract the carrying trade from the Dutch, Stebbing's Ralegh, p. 268. Vide also the following abstracts from Raleigh's works. The works of Sir Walter Ralegh (Lond., 1751), ii, p. 87: "there are five manifest Causes of the Upgrowing of the Hollanders and Zealanders." Ibid., p. 114: "To bring this to pass they have many Advantages of us; the one is, by their fashioned ships called Boyers, Hoybarks, Hoys, and others that are made to hold great Bulk of Merchandise, used to sail with a few Men for Profit. For Example, though an English ship of two hundred Tons, and a Holland Ship, or any other of the petty States of the same Burden be at Dantzick, or any other Place beyond the Seas or in England, they do serve the Merchant better cheap by one hundred Pounds in his Freight than we can, by reason he hath but nine or ten Mariners, and we over thirty." Cf. ibid., p. 118. Ibid., p. 123: "Notwithstanding the Low-Countries have as many Ships and Vessels as eleven Kingdoms of Christendom have."

English colonies of Virginia and Barbadoes.[1] " Low interest
and low customs, says Sir Josiah Child, were the reason
why, before the Act of Navigation, there went ten Dutch
ships to Barbadoes for one English."[2] After the execution
of Charles I. Virginia passed an Act declaring the execution
and trial to be treason, and asserting that Charles II. was the
legitimate king.[3] In Barbadoes the course of events was
similar,[4] and a resolution was adopted to give the Dutch the
preference in commerce.[5] The answer of parliament came in
the celebrated act of October, 1650.[6] Two most important
enactments are contained in this ordinance. One was that
all who had been guilty of the acts mentioned above[7] were

[1] Sir Robert H. Schomburgk, (Lond., 1848), *History of Barbados*, pp. 268,
272; Ranke, *History of England*, iii, p. 8.

[2] *A New Discourse of Trade*, pp. 195, 196. For low interest, *cf.* J. de Witt,
The True Interest and Political Maxims (Lond., 1746), p. 285.

[3] Hening, i, pp. 359–361.

[4] Sainsbury, *Calendar*, 1661–1668, p. 541; Edwards, *History of the West Indies*,
i, pp. 348, 349; Sainsbury's *Calendar*, 1584–1660, pp. 342, 343, 350, 390.

[5] Ranke, iii, p. 68. After the execution of the king, many who had been officers
in his army went to Barbadoes and other islands, where they became planters; *cf.*
Campbell, *Sugar Trade*, p. 63.

[6] This is for our purpose the most important act passed under the commonwealth. The full text may be found in Scobell's *Collection of Acts and Ordinances* (Lond., 1658), ii, pp. 132–134. Brief and garbled outlines may be
found in Hazard, i, p. 638; Cobbett, *Parliamentary History*, iii, p. 1357;
Whitelocke's *Memorials*, p. 458; Anderson, ii, p. 546; Bozman's *Maryland*, ii, pp.
413, 414 n.; Macpherson, ii, p. 439; Chalmers' *Political Annals*, pp. 122, 123.
Reeves' *Law of Shipping*, pp. 34–36, gives an excellent outline. For orders to
the generals at sea for the execution of this act, *vide* Sainsbury's *Calendar*, 1584–
1660, pp. 344, 361. For a license to trade contrary to this act, *cf. ibid.*, p. 356.

[7] " And whereas divers acts of Rebellion have been committed by many persons
inhabiting on Barbada's, Antego, Bermuda's and Virginia, whereby they have
most Trayterously, by Force and Subtility, usurped a Power of Government, and
seized the Estates of many well-affected persons into their hands, and banished
others, and have set up themselves in opposition to, and distinct from this State
and Commonwealth, many of the chief Actors in, and Promotors of these Re-
bellions having been transported and carried over to the said Plantations in
Foreign Ships, without leave, license or consent of the Parliament of England."
Scobell, ii, p. 132.

declared to be " notorious Robbers and Traitors," and therefore by " the Law of Nations " they were forbidden to have
" any maner of Commerce or Traffique with any people whatsoever." [1]

The Council of State was, however, given the power to
grant leave and license to any of the ships of England to
visit and trade with these colonies.[2]   The general court of
Massachusetts thereupon passed a law forbidding all trade
with Virginia.[3]   When Virginia surrendered to parliament in
March of this year it was provided in one of the articles of
the surrender that her people should enjoy their former trade
privileges.[4]   Massachusetts then repealed the above mentioned law.[5]

There was another provision in the ordinance, of broader
scope and of more permanent effect.   In order to prevent
foreign ships carrying enemies of parliament to the colonies,
all such vessels were forbidden to trade with the colonies
unless under special license.[6]

While the relation of the Dutch to these events in the
colonies was paving the way for a quarrel between England
and the States-General, other events nearer home were tend-
ing to the same result.   In the first place parliament felt

---

[1] Scobell, ii, p. 132.   [2] *Ibid.*, p. 134.   [3] Hazard, i, p. 561.

[4] Hening, i, p. 364, Article 7. "That the people of Virginia have free trade as
the people of England do enjoy to all places and with all nations according to
the lawes of that commonwealth, and that Virginia shall enjoy all priviledges
equall with any English plantations in America." *Cf.* also Hazard, i, p. 561.

[5] Hazard, i, p. 558, 14 October, 1651.

[6] "And to prevent for the time to come, and to hinder the carrying over of any
such persons as are Enemies to this Commonwealth, or that may prove dangerous
to any of the English Plantations in America, the Parliament doth forbid and
prohibit all ships of any Foreign Nation, whatsoever, to come to, or Trade in, or
Traffique with any of the English Plantations in America, or any Islands, Ports, or
places thereof, which are planted by, and in possession of the People of this
Commonwealth, without License first had and obtained from the Parliament or
Council of State." Scobell, ii, p. 133.

strong "resentment" because of "the execrable Murther committed here, upon the Person of Doctor Dorislaus."[1] Then Oliver St. John's mission had been unsuccessful, and the proposal for a union of the two countries had been rejected.[2] The anger caused by these acts, and the relations of the Dutch to colonial commerce, were the occasion of the passage of the famous Navigation Act. The cause may be found in England's jealousy of Dutch commercial and maritime supremacy.[3]

In October, 1651, this famous act was passed. Its main provisions are as follows:

I. No goods of the growth or manufacture of Asia, Africa, or America shall be imported into England or the dominions thereof, except in ships of which the proprietor, master and the major part of the mariners are English.[4]

II. No goods of the growth or manufacture of Europe, shall be imported into England or the dominions thereof, except in English ships and in such foreign ships as do belong to that country where the goods are produced and manufactured.

III. No goods of foreign growth or manufacture, that are to be brought into England, shall be brought from any other place than the place of growth or production, or from those

[1] Rymer, xx, p. 596; Thurloe, *State Papers*, i, p. 174.

[2] Thurloe, i, pp. 182–195; Rymer, xx, p. 600, *et seq.;* de Wicquefort, *L'Histoire des Provinces Unies* (1743), ii, pp. 287–294.

[3] Green views the question from a totally different standpoint. "But it was necessary for Vane's purposes not only to show the energy of the Parliament, but to free it from the control of the army. His aim was to raise in the navy a force devoted to the House, and to eclipse the glories of Dunbar and Worcester by yet greater triumphs at sea. With this view the quarrel with Holland had been carefully nursed; a 'Navigation Act,' prohibiting the importation, etc." *History of the English People*, iii, p. 275.

[4] A full text is in Scobell, ii, pp. 176–177; an outline, with important provisions omitted, in Cobbett's *Parliamentary History*, iii, p. 1374; an outline with errors in Anderson, ii, pp. 550, 551.

ports where alone the goods can be shipped, or whence they are usually first shipped after transportation.

There were also some minor provisions and some exceptions. The penalty for the violation of the act was confiscation both of the cargo and the vessel.

As can be readily seen, this statute was aimed especially against the vast carrying trade of the Dutch. Against the ordinance of 1650, and the act of 1651, the Dutch petitioned in vain.[1] The ill feeling engendered ultimately led to a naval war in which the two great admirals, Blake and Van Tromp, contended for the mastery.

It will now be interesting to see how these two important acts were executed. Sir Francis Brewster, writing a generation later, says, "for it is to be observed, That under Oliver's Government, the Act of Navigation had little force; both Government, and the merchants, were willing to let it sleep."[2] In New England the regulations do not seem to have been enforced.[3] Hutchinson speaks of the trade of Massachusetts in 1655 as flourishing. Admission to vessels of all nations was free; ships of the colony traded to and from France, Holland and other countries.[4] In Virginia the acts seem to have been more strictly executed. This was undoubtedly due to the strength of the Cavalier party in this colony.

In 1651, the English ambassador at the Hague wrote to the council of state: "Diverse merchants ships have lately arrived in this countrye from the Caribbee Islands and Virginia, and four are provideinge for the Caribbee Islands from Amsterdam, Horne, Memlicke, and Edam in these parts.

[1] *New York Colonial Documents*, i, p. 436; p. 486.

[2] *Essays on Trade and Navigation* (London, 1695), p. 101.

[3] Palfrey's *New England*, ii, p. 393.

[4] Hutchinson, *History of Massachusetts* (Salem, 1795), i, p. 174. In 1655 two ships, that had been seized at Plymouth for trading with the English plantations in America, were released, Sainsbury's *Calendar*, 1584–1660, p. 423.

We shall hereafter give you the names of these ships. Very lately your ships took two Dutch ships, the Blew Unicorne and the Mary, which were bound for the Barbadoes."[1] In 1652, a petition was presented to the Council of State for the restitution of several hogsheads of tobacco seized in a Dutch vessel coming from Virginia.[2] In 1653, the ship "Leopoldus" of Dunkirk was confiscated in Virginia for a breach of the acts.[3]

Still even in Virginia the acts were not executed very stringently, especially after the peace with Holland. Thus in 1655 the statement was made that "divers ships are usually found intruding at Virginia, and surreptitiously carrying away the growth of the plantation to foreign parts."[4] Cromwell was apt to condone violations, if his position in foreign politics might thereby become more commanding. An instance of this is furnished by the treaty which in 1656 the commissioners of the Commonwealth signed with Charles Gustavus of Sweden. One of the articles contained the statement that, if any of the Swedish subjects should privately solicit license to trade with the colonies in America, the Lord Protector would as far as possible comply with the desires of the Swedish King.[5] In 1656, a

---

[1] Thurloe, *State Papers* (London, 1742), i, p. 187. In 1651 Sir George Ayscue wrote he "has taken, since his last letters, a Dutch brig and a Dutch vessel of 16 guns, bound to Barbadoes with horses, beer, and other provisions, making in all 14, which if possible will be sold." Sainsbury, *Calendar*, 1584-1660, p. 364. We hear of the seizure in 1658 of several Dutch ships trading at Barbadoes, *ibid.*, p. 467.

[2] Sainsbury, *Calendar*, 1584-1660, p. 395; *cf.* also, p. 403; p. 405.

[3] Hening, i, pp. 382, 382 n. Hening's statement, i, p. 513 n., that the acts were not at all enforced seems to me, in view of the above facts, to be exaggerated. In 1654 we find two petitions that were presented, one to Cromwell, the other to the Council of State, for licenses to ship goods from Amsterdam direct to Virginia, Sainsbury, 1584-1660, pp. 418, 419.

[4] Sainsbury, *Calendar*, 1584-1660, p. 420.

[5] J. du Mont, *Corps Universel Diplomatique*, (Amst., 1728), vi, parts ii and iii,

petition against the acts of 1650 and 1651 was sent to England by Virginia. The colonists claimed that the cessation of trade with the Dutch would ruin them, and that they were forced to trade secretly with the Dutch.[1] The Virginians also claimed a legal exemption from the acts. They said that the article in the surrender freed them not only from the first provision of the ordinance of 1650, but also from the second.[2] In accord with these views in 1659–60, an act was passed in Virginia, stating that the Dutch and all strangers of any Christian nation in amity with the people of England had full liberty to trade with this colony, for all allowable commodities.[3]

p. 127. " *Quod ad commercium in America habendum id quidem lege diserte cautum est, ne cujus vis praeterea Reipublicae Subditis sine peculiari licentia Commercium illic, promiscue habendi potestas fiat, siquis autem Subditorum Serenissimi Regis Sueciae, ejusdem Literis commendatitiis munitus, hanc sibi licentiam privatim ad eas quaslibet colonias petiverit, Dominus Protector, quoad rerum ac Reipublicae status pro tempore permiserit, haud invitus hac in parte desiderio Serenissimae Regiae Majestatis Sueciae satisfaciat.*" This may be found translated in Hazard, i, p. 605; also in Anderson, ii, p. 583.

[1] Hazard, i, pp. 559–601.

[2] Hening, i, p. 535, Act. ix, 1659–60. The words seem to justify the assumption of the Virginians.

[3] Hening, i, p. 450.

CHAPTER II. THE ACTS OF CHARLES II. AND THE BASIS OF THE COLONIAL SYSTEM.[1]

§ 1. *Introduction.* In the first chapter the growth of the policy of protection to home shipping was traced. From the days of the son of the Black Prince a nearly continuous succession of statutes shows how familiar this policy was to English statesmen. The policy reached its culmination in the celebrated act of Cromwell.

Side by side with this we traced the development of the ultimate cause which led Englishmen, as well as other Europeans, to voyages of discovery and then to colonization. The motive which induced the government of England to aid colonization was hope of gain. At first it was hope of gain expressed in the search for precious metals, but finally it developed into the theory of commercial monopoly held under the later Stuarts. From these two lines of policy developed the colonial system of England. The trade of the colonies was reserved to English and colonial shipping; the colonist had to sell and buy in the home market, and thus was the weaker party in nearly all transactions.

During the reigns of James I. and Charles I. we saw germs of this home market theory, but no definite policy had been adopted. During that period we even find a statement like the following: " It was a Liberty and Privilege, generally taken and enjoyed, by all his Majesty's Subjects, to carry their Commodities to the best Markets." [2] The policy of the first two Stuarts was influenced by subjective considerations and by the chances of foreign politics. The policy inaugurated

---

[1] Forster's *Digest* (Lond., 1727), pp. 89–105. [2] Stith, p. 201.

by Charles II. differs greatly from that of his predecessors. In it economic, not political and moral, considerations were the controlling factors. If the King prohibits the growth of tobacco in England, it is not because English tobacco is unhealthy, but because by so doing he gives his colony a monopoly in return for confining the colonial tobacco trade to the home market.

The two lines of policy, that of protecting English and colonial shipping, and that of so regulating the trade of the colonies that they might contribute to the benent of the mother country, were combined in the acts of Charles II. For the first time a policy definite and uniform for all the colonies was evolved. Thus, in 1660, the famous "Act for the Encouraging and Increasing of Shipping and Navigation" was passed, and later during this reign, other statutes of similar import were enacted.

§ 2. *Protection to Shipping.* The provisions of the act of 1660 affecting shipping were as follows:

I. No goods should be imported into or exported from any plantations belonging to his Majesty in Asia, Africa or America, unless in ships which truly belonged to and were built by, the people of England, Ireland, Wales Berwick, or any of the plantations. The master and three-quarters of the crew of such vessels must be English.[1]

II. Goods of the growth, production or manufacture of Africa, Asia or America should not be imported into England, except in ships navigated, built, and owned as decribed above.[2]

III. No goods of foreign growth or manufacture should be imported into England, Ireland, Wales, Guernsey, Jersey, or Berwick, unless they come directly from the place of growth or production, or from those ports whence the goods and commodities were usually shipped.[3]

---

[1] 12 Charles II., c. 18, § i.   [2] *Ibid.*, § iii.

[3] From this point we shall no longer discuss the policy of England as regards

This provided for the monopoly of the carrying trade between England and the colonies. But merchants as distinct from ship-owners would receive no benefit from this act; something must, therefore, be done to placate them.

In mediæval England staple towns had been created, such as Calais. "The merchants of the staple had a monopoly of purchase and export."[2] The English merchant now asked whether it would not be good for him to make England the staple for the colonies. He, like the old staplers, would then have the monopoly of exporting the commodities of England and of Europe to the colonies.

In accordance with these views, a statute was passed three years later making England the staple, "not only of the Commodities of those Plantations, but also of the Commodities of other Countries and Places, for the supplying of them." Under the provisions of this act commodities of the growth or manufacture of Europe must be laden and shipped in England, Wales or Berwick for exportation to America. None but "English built" shipping, navigated according to law, could carry these commodities to the colonies.[3]

There were some exceptions to the rigidity of the law in favor of certain industries. Salt for the fisheries of New England and Newfoundland could be imported directly from any port of Europe.[4] Later Pennsylvania[5] and then New York[6] received the same privilege. Wines could be sent directly from Madeira and Azores. There was some doubt

protection to English navigation proper, except where it influences the colonial policy, and where it is necessary to a clear comprehension of the same.

[1] Low and Pulling, *Dictionary of English History*, p. 968; Hall, *The Customs-Revenue*, ii, pp. 121–127; Gross, *The Gild Merchant*, i, p. 140; Ochenkowski, *England's Wirtschaftliche Entwickelung*, p. 187; Anderson, ii, p. 618; Longman, *Edward III.*, i, pp. 340, 341; Ashley, *Introduction to English Economic History*, i, p. 111.

[2] Stubbs, *Constitutional History of England*, ii. p. 411.

[3] 15 Charles II., c. vii, § vi.   [4] *Ibid.*, § vii.   [5] 13 Geo. I., c. 5.   [6] 3 Geo. II., c. 12.

as to whether the Canary Isles were included in this category, for the provision mentions Azores and Madeira, but omits any mention of the Canaries.[1] It was, however, customary to allow wines to be imported directly from them, because they formed a part of the larger group know as the Western Islands.[2] Provisions, horses and servants from Ireland and Scotland were included in the same category. In Anne's reign the Irish were allowed to export their linen directly to America.[3]

§ 3. *Restriction of Trade to the Home Market.* The act of 1660 provided that certain articles should not be exported except to England and to the other colonies. These were sugar, tobacco, cotton-wool, indigo, ginger, fustic, and other dyeing woods.[4] It will be seen that these commodities were the products of the West Indies and of the Southern colonies. Tobacco was the only preëminently continental product. On the other hand the Northern colonies could export their grain, fish and naval stores whithersoever their economic advantage led them. Ships sailing from the colonies with any of these commodities on board had to give bond to land the same at some port of England, Ireland or Wales.[5]

[1] 15 Charles II., c. 1, § vii, says "Western Islands of Azores." The Western islands included the Canary, Azores and Madeira islands, 12 Charles II., c. 18, § xiv.

[2] Mr. Fane, in 1736–7, said that the Canary islands were included in the permission to export wines directly, both from long usage and because "I apprehend that the Canary Islands are not esteemed, by books of geography, to be a part of Europe, and consequently the importation of the wines directly to New York and New England, will not be considered as a breach of the above-mentioned act of parliament." Chalmers, *Opinions of Eminent Lawyers* (Lond., 1814), ii, pp. 275, 276. Governor Bernard thinks that Portugal ought to have enjoyed the same privilege; that it was a "casus omissus in the letter of the Law," *Select Letters*, pp. 2, 3. The explanation of the distinction is probably to be found in the great distance of these islands from England, and their geographical separation from Europe.

[3] 3 and 4 Anne, c. 8, § 1; 3 Geo. I., c. 21, § 1.   [4] 12 Charles II. c. 18, § xviii.

[5] 12 Charles II., c. 18, § xix. For further provisions as regards bonds see Sains-

The colonist was allowed to export these commodities to other plantations, and from these plantations it was possible to export them to the countries of the European continent.

In 1662 it appeared that the statute was evaded in three ways; by delivering tobacco to the Dutch at sea, by carrying tobacco to New England and thence shipping it in Dutch bottoms to Europe, and by direct shipment to the Dutch plantations.[1] The farmers of the customs in 1663 complained that this direct trade with the Dutch caused a loss to the revenue of £10,000 a year.[2] Moreover the products sent through England had paid duties, and the illegal trader was thus enabled to undersell the English merchant in the European markets. To remedy the harm to the customs a statute was passed in 1672. It provided that if the merchant refused to give bond that he would bring the enumerated commodities to England, saying that he was going to take them to some other colony, the following duties should be imposed:[3]

1. Sugar (white)...............................5 sh.   a cwt.
2. Sugar (brown and muscavado) ....1 sh. 6 d. a cwt.
3. Tobacco...................................1 d.   a lb.
4. Cotton-wool ....½ d.   a lb.
5. Ginger...................................1 sh.   a cwt.
6. Logwood..................................5 £   a cwt.
7. Fustic ....6 d.   a cwt.

The duties were to be levied in the plantations by the commissioner of the customs in England,[4] and were to be paid into the British Exchequer.[5]

bury, *Calendar*, 1661–1668, pp. 10, 11; *Massachusetts Historical Society Collections*, 4th series, ii, p. 279; 7 and 8 Will. III., c. 22, § xiii; 8 Anne, c. 13, § xxiii. To prevent violations 22 and 23 Charles II., c. 26, § xii, provided that the governors were to hand once a year to the officers of the customs of London a list of all ships and of all bonds taken to bring these commodities to their legal destination.

[1] *New York Colonial Documents*, iii, p. 44.

[2] Sainsbury, *Calendar*, 1661–68, p. 172; *New York Colonial Documents*, iii, p. 47; pp. 48, 49; *cf.* also p. 103 and p. 106 of Sainsbury's *Calendar*, 1661–1668.

[3] 25 Charles II., c. 7, § ii.   [4] *Ibid.*, § iii.   [5] 1 Geo. I., *Stat.* 2, c. 12, § 4.

The colonists considered that, after paying the duty, they might export the goods to any port in Europe. Attorney-General Jones, however, in 1675, said that the tax must be paid and security also given to carry the productions to a dominion of the crown, because the law imposing the duties did not repeal that requiring the bond.[1] James II. was of the same opinion. To Governor Dongan he wrote, in 1686, "you are to understand, That the payment of the said Rates and Dutys . . . doth not give liberty to carry the said goods to any other place than to some other of our Plantations or to England, Wales or Berwick."[2]   In the reign of William and Mary it was expressly enacted that none of these goods could be re-shipped unless bond were given as provided in the act of 1660.[3]   And if these commodities were so shipped, on arrival in England, they had to pay the regular duties.[4]

§ 4. *Minor Regulations.*   It should be kept in mind that these acts were not binding on Scotland, for the relation between England and Scotland was then merely a personal one.   Thus in 1661 the Scotch Parliament passed an "act for encourageing of Shiping and Navigation."[5]   The wording and provisions are nearly identical with those of the English act of 1660.   So the Scotch were not allowed to trade with

[1] Chalmers, *Political Annals*, p. 319; pp. 323, 324.

[2] *New York Colonial Documents*, iii, p. 384; *cf.* also the instructions to Edward Randolph in 1678 in *Massachusetts Historical Society Collections*, 3d series, vii, pp. 132, 133.

[3] 7 and 8 Will. III., c. 22, § viii.

[4] *Andros Tracts* (Prince Society Public.), ii, pp. 129, 130.   Simon Bradstreet wrote from Boston in 1680, " what they carry from hence, the full custome is payd att the place from whence they first bring them, being the groath of some other of his ma'ties plantacons, and if they carry them to England, which generly is done, they pay the Custome againe."   *Massachusetts Historical Society Collections*, 3rd series, viii, p. 331.

[5] *Acts of the Parliament of Scotland* (1820), vii, p. 257.

the English plantations, since "they are strangers."[1]   Still
occasionally licenses were granted permitting Scotchmen to
trade with the American colonies.   In 1663 we find a license
to John Brown to trade with four Scotch ships to the colonies, "provided the said Ships return directly into Scotland
or England."[2]   The next year the license was renewed.[3]   In
1669, on petition of the Duke of York, an order in council
was issued granting a license to two Scotch ships to trade
and fish in the colony of New York.[4]   Against this license
the farmers of the customs petitioned most strenuously.[5]

Another problem has also to be answered, *viz.*, could
Scotchmen be counted to make up the proportion of English sailors required on the crew of every vessel navigated
according to law?   Chalmers[6] says they could, and he relies
for his assertion on the decision of Coke in regard to the
naturalization of persons born in Scotland after the accession
of James to the English throne.   This view seems wholly
untenable.   A statute of Charles II. says, "it is to be understood, that any of his Majesty's Subjects of England, Ireland,
and his Plantations, are to be accounted English, and no
others."[7]   James also wrote to Governor Dongan, "you are
to understand, that any of our subjects of England Ireland
or the Plantations are to be accounted English and noe others."[8]   That is, previous to 1707, inhabitants of England,
Wales, Berwick,[9] Ireland, or the plantations, were English,
but Scotchmen were strangers.   The Act of Union, however,

---

[1] Sainsbury, *Calendar*, 1661–1668, p. 58, p. 156.

[2] *Ibid.* (Aug. 25th, 1663), p. 156.   [3] *Ibid.* (Nov. 13th, 1664), p. 254.

[4] *New York Colonial Documents*, iii, p. 180.   [5] *Ibid.*, iii, pp. 180, 181.

[6] *Political Annals*, p. 258.   [7] 13 and 14 Charles II., c. 11, § vi.

[8] *New York Colonial Documents*, iii, p. 383.

[9] 20 Geo. II., c. 42, § iii.   In all cases where England is mentioned in an act of
parliament, Wales and Berwick were included.   *Cf.* also *Rex vs. Cowle*, 2 *Bur-
rows*, pp. 847, 853.

abolished all such differences between Englishmen and Scotchmen.[1]

We have seen above stated that by the act of 1660, enumerated goods could be imported directly into Ireland. But the word Ireland seems to have been placed there merely by inadvertence. For in 15 Charles II., c. 7, § 2, we find that goods could not be shipped from Ireland to the colonies, but only from England, Wales, or Berwick. By a later statute (1670), it was expressly enacted that the word "Ireland" be left out of the bonds, meaning that enumerated goods could no longer be sent directly thither.[2] In 1695, the merchants of Bristol complained of the immense trade between the plantations and Ireland and Scotland, saying that the revenue suffered a yearly loss of £50,000 thereby.[3] Accordingly, the next year the colonies were prohibited from sending even the non-enumerated commodities to Ireland. All commodities had to be sent to England, and after the duties were paid could then be sent to Ireland.[4] But by a statute passed in George II.'s reign, it was finally provided that the non-enumerated commodities could be sent directly to Ireland.[5]

One other provision in the act of 1660 is worthy of mention. By clause 18, section 2 of this statute, aliens were forbidden to exercise the business of merchants or factors in the colonies. The provision was aimed against the Dutch merchants who were resident there.[6]

[1] 5 Anne, c. 8, § iv.

[2] 22 and 23 Charles II., c. 26, § ii; *cf.* also *Massachusetts Historical Society Collections*, 3d series, vii, p. 136.   [3] Chalmers, *Revolt*, i, p. 269, p. 260.

[4] 7 and 8 Will. III., c. 22, § xiv.   [5] 4 Geo. II., c. 15; as regards hops, 5 Geo. II., c. 9.

[6] Anderson, ii, p. 599. Doyle in *"English in America,"* (*Southern Colonies*), p. 308, makes a curious blunder. He says this act "forbade *any man* to establish himself as a merchant or factor in the colonies." Prof. Fisher of Yale copies this error in nearly identical language. He says (*Colonial Era*, p. 51), " *no man* was to be allowed to establish himself as a merchant or factor in the colonies."

CHAPTER III.   A HISTORY OF THE ENUMERATED COMMODITIES, 1660-1763.

§ 1. *Economic Principle.*   The economic principle that governed the acts of the English statesmen during the seventeenth and eighteenth centuries was that of the mercantile system.   This system laid especial stress on the balance of trade and the possession of the precious metals.   Legislation must be devoted to increasing the amount of commodities exported and decreasing the amount of commodities imported.   Thereby the *summum bonum* would be obtained; gold and silver would flow into the country.   One way to increase the exports and to obtain a favorable balance of trade would be for a country to engage extensively in manufactures.   Thus some source of supply for raw materials was needed.

If now England should import her raw materials from foreign countries, she would probably have to pay for the same in money, since the mercantile system obtained in other countries as well as in England.   If England imported the raw materials from her colonies she could pay for the same in manufactures; the precious metals would not be drained from England, but might even flow thither from the colonies.   The question whether the balance of trade was unfavorable to both England and the colonies, regarded as a unit, affected the economists and statesmen but little.   What they sought was a favorable balance for England alone.   This standpoint was natural.   Although Bodinus[1] had already

[1] Bodini, *De Republica* (Frankfort, 1541), Book i, chap. viii, p. 123, *"De iure maiestatis";* Baudrillart, *Bodin et son Temps,* p. 267.

clearly pointed out the distinction between sovereignty and government, his theories had by no means taken a firm foot-hold. The colonies were not regarded as integral members of the English state from the very fact that, territorially (in those days of sailing vessels), they were so far removed, and especially because their connection with the English government was so loose. Colonies were then (as even frequently now)[1] regarded not as component parts of a state, but as pos-sessions of the state, to be administered for the state's benefit. Due to the fluctuating views held on this point, the colonies occupied a rather anomalous position. In matters of trade we find the colonies on one occasion treated as if they were for-eign countries, and on another as if they were parts of the English state.

Thus the colonies were to be the source of England's raw materials, and the vent of England's manufactures. If the colonists could send their raw materials to a foreign country, of what benefit would it be for England to have colonies? Other nations would gain the same benefit from England's colonies, without having incurred the expense of establishing and protecting them. To gain the full benefit from the possession of colonies, the exportation of these raw materials and articles of immediate consumption must be limited to the home market. Thus we have seen that, in 1660, it was enacted that ginger, sugar, tobacco, cotton-wool, indigo, fustic and other dyeing woods had to be sent to England or to some other plantation. None of these commodities, ex-cept tobacco, could be raised in England, and the produc-tion of tobacco was forbidden. These commodities were the products of the West India islands and of Virginia. The staple articles of New England were not enumerated, because they could be produced in England. As the industries of

[1] *Vide* Seeley's brilliant book, *The Expansion of England.*

England increased, other commodities, that were not enumerated in 1660, had to be imported in large quantities,
since England could not produce them in quantities sufficient
for her manufactures. Thus gradually other commodities
were added to the list. These commodities had, however,
to pay heavy duties when imported into England, and thus
the English producer was saved from ruinous competition.

This brings us to the other purpose for which commodities were enumerated. They had all, on importation, to pay
heavy duties, and it was hoped that these indirect taxes
would be very lucrative.

In the following sections, we shall show what changes
were made in the list of enumerated articles, what commodities were added to the original list, and what special privileges were granted to certain commodities.[1]

§ 2. *Tobacco.* In a preceding section we saw how James
I. and Charles I. had prohibited the growth of tobacco in
England, and had given advantages to colonial over Spanish
tobacco. Cromwell pursued the same policy.[2] In 1652, he
caused, by act of parliament, the growth of tobacco in England to be prohibited, and later he appointed commissioners
to see that the act was strictly executed.[3] The excise which
he imposed was one shilling on foreign tobacco and one
penny on plantation tobacco.[4] Virginia herself led up to the
policy of enumeration by an act passed in 1659–60.[5] All

---

[1] The history of the purely continental products will be given, together with an
account of those among West Indian products, which had a vital influence on the
development of the continental colonies. Thus indigo, which only began to be
produced extensively on the continent at the middle of the eighteenth century,
will not be discussed here, but under the head of bounties.

[2] Sainsbury, *Calendar,* 1584–1660, pp. 403, 405, 415, 417, 422, 423, 424, 466;
Anderson, ii, p. 557; Holmes, *Annals of America,* i, p. 296.

[3] Anderson, ii, p. 557.

[4] *An Additional Act* (London, 1657), p. 2; Dowell, ii, p. 12; iv, p. 270.

[5] Hening, i, pp. 536, 537.

merchants, unless trading in ships belonging to Virginians, had under that statute to pay on every hogshead of tobacco sent to any place in Europe, except England, ten shillings.

While in the policy of Charles II. toward tobacco we shall find no novel elements, yet there is an important difference between his policy and that of his predecessors. This policy is founded on a broader basis. No longer do we find the king attempting to make a royal monopoly of tobacco. The people of England are to have this monopoly. Discriminations are no longer made against Spanish tobacco on account of the King's personal pique, but in order that the colonists may have a monopoly of the English market.

The belief still lingered on that the use of tobacco was immoral, and that the existence of a colony relying on the production of such a commodity must be precarious. We continually find exhortations and remonstrances of Charles to Virginia, that tobacco should be abandoned for hemp, flax and silk. In 1662 some merchants and planters of Virginia petitioned that the planting of tobacco in Virginia and Maryland be prohibited, in order that the production of silk, hemp, flax, pitch and potashes might be encouraged.[1] A little later the King commanded Sir William Berkeley to promote the staple commodities mentioned in the petition above, and also masts and timber.[2] These attempts all ended in failure, because the Virginians and Marylanders saw that the production of tobacco conduced to their economic advantage.

In 1660, tobacco was enumerated, and in return the production of tobacco in England was prohibited. Since tobacco is one of the main products of the plantations, says the statute, and since by planting in England his Majesty's revenues are decreased, the planting of tobacco in England,

---

[1] Sainsbury (1661–1668), p. 90.   [2] *Ibid.*, p. 99; *cf.* p. 103; *cf.* p. 110.

Ireland or Wales is forbidden.[1]   One half a pole may be
planted in the "physick garden" of either university, or in
any private garden devoted to scientific purposes.[2]   The
penalties imposed proved too small, and three years later
they were increased five-fold.[3]   Later, since tobacco still
continued to be planted in England, to the detriment of the
customs, the plantations, and navigation and trade, severer
regulations were introduced.   Justices of the peace were to
issue warrants to all constables, petty constables and tithing-
men, to find out what tobacco was planted, and all these
officers, then, on warrant of two or more justices of the
peace, were to pull up and destroy all such tobacco.[4]   The
numerous prohibitions of the growth of tobacco in England,
show that its cultivation was very profitable.[5]   While on
the one hand colonial tobacco was limited to the home
market, the Englishman was forbidden to grow his own
supply, but had to buy it instead from the colonial producer.

The colonists would not have a complete monopoly of the
home market unless Spanish tobacco were excluded by very
high duties.[6]   In the "Old Subsidy"[7] of five per cent. in
1660 Spanish and Brazilian tobacco was rated at ten shillings,
plantation tobacco at one shilling eight pence.   That is, foreign tobacco paid six pence a pound, colonial tobacco one

---

[1] 12 Charles II., c. 34, § i;   confirmed by 13 Charles II., *Stat.* i, c. 14.

[2] *Ibid.*, § iv;   15 Charles II., c. 7, § xx.   [3] 15 Charles II., c. 7, § xviii.

[4] 22 and 23 Charles II., c. 26, § i, § ii, § iv.

[5] For tobacco in England, *cf. The True English Interest* of Carew Reynell,
1674, in *Scarce Tracts on Trade and Commerce* of Sir Charles Whitworth, London, 1778, p. 163; Rogers, *Economic Interpretation of History*, p. 322, says: "It
appears to have been cultivated in the midland counties, and particularly in Glou-
cestershire."   In Sainsbury's *Calendar*, 1584–1660, p. 405, Worcester, Gloucester,
Somerset and Hereford are mentioned.

[6] For the duties on tobacco, *vide* Saxby, *The British Customs* (London, 1757),
pp. 9, 10, 12, 15, 21, 23, 24, 28, 29, 30, 244, 245, 246.

[7] 12 Charles II., c. 4.

penny a pound. There was likewise an additional duty of
one penny a pound on plantation tobacco, but on reëxportation within a year this additional duty was to be repaid.
One-half of the subsidy was repaid if tobacco was reëxported
within a year by an Englishman, and within nine months by
a foreigner.[1]

Under James the duties were considerably increased. In
addition to the former duties colonial tobacco had to pay
three pence a pound and foreign tobacco six pence a pound.[2]
If reëxported within a year and a half the whole duty was
epaid.[3] By the " New Subsidy "[4] of William III. an additional five per cent. was charged, or one penny a pound.
This was repaid on reëxportation.[5] By the " One-Third
Subsidy "[6] of Anne, an additional one-third penny was
charged per pound, and this was all repaid on reëxportation.[7]
Thus in Anne's reign the duties amounted to six and one-
third pence per pound on colonial tobacco, and the drawback was five and five-sixths pence. The duties on foreign
tobacco amounted to twenty pence. Finally, under George
I., the time for reëxportation was extended to three years,[8]
and the whole duty on colonial tobacco was repaid on re-
exportation.[9] By the " Subsidy of 1747 "[10] one penny additional was charged on colonial, and six pence on Spanish
and Brazilian tobacco. The drawback amounted to the
whole duty.[11]

From this brief summary it will be seen, that Spanish

---

[1] 2nd rule of the Book of Rates. We shall not discuss the various rebates for
cash payment, and payments within certain periods. They can all be found in
Saxby, and if introduced into the text would create useless confusion.

[2] 1 James. II., c. 4, § i.

[3] Ibid., § vii.

[4] 9 and 10 Wm. III., c. 23, § iv.

[5] Ibid., § xiii.

[6] 2 and 3 Ann., c. 9, § 1.

[7] Ibid., § ii.

[8] 1 Geo. I., Stat. 1, c. 21, § x.

[9] 9 Geo. I., c. 21, § vi.

[10] 21 Geo. II., c. 2.

[11] Ibid., § v, § vi.

tobacco was discriminated against to a considerable extent. The duties paid were three times as high as those on colonial tobacco, and this fact, in addition to the high price of Spanish tobacco, gave the colonist a practical monopoly of the English market.[1]

The price of tobacco fell gradually, but constantly, during the 17th century. In 1619, tobacco was worth three shillings a pound; in 1704, two pence a pound.[2] But at the former date, only 20,000 pounds of tobacco were exported from Virginia, and naturally none from Maryland; while at the latter date 18,295,000 pounds were sent from Virginia alone.[3] Davenant, in a report to the commissioner of accounts, gives the imports of tobacco into England, on an average of ten years, ending in 1709, as 28,858,666 pounds.[4] That is, the price had declined to one-eighteenth of what it was, the quantity exported had increased nearly fifteen hundred times. This great increase in the supply, with a slower increase in the demand, tended, most naturally, to a decline in prices. We have other, besides statistical evidence, of a great increase in supply. Tobacco was overproduced in Virginia, and the planters agreed to stop planting in 1667.[5] The celebrated mercantilist, Joshua Gee, tells us, that on one occasion, when the market was overstocked with tobacco,

---

[1] Numerous administrative statutes were passed to prevent smuggling and getting a larger drawback than was due. No drawback to be allowed for tobacco, exported in a ship under 20 tons, 8 Anne, c. 13, § xx; no drawback was allowed for tobacco exported in any package but casks of 300 lbs., 9 Geo. I., c. 21, § xiv; no drawback was paid unless tobacco were shipped from the port at which imported and in the original package, 24 Geo. II., c. 41, § iv; no tobacco to be exported unless in casks of 425 pounds or more, and none to be exported unless in vessels of 70 tons, except to Ireland, 24 Geo. II., c. 41, § xxv. For a complete list of these regulations compare *Index to Statutes at Large* under Tobacco, and *Saxby*, pp. 605–618.

[2] Brock, p. 224.   [3] *Ibid.*

[4] *Works* of D'avenant (London, 1771), v, p. 427; Brock, p. 218.

[5] Sainsbury, 1661–1668, p. 446; *cf.* also 513.

the crown bought the product and subsequently had it burned.[1]

The heavy and excessive duties mentioned above, naturally strengthened the tendency to a fall in prices. For on comparing them with the fluctuating prices of tobacco, it will be seen that they amounted to from 100 per cent. to 250 per cent. *ad valorem*. Against such heavy duties the planters protested, and in 1733 their complaints were embodied in a short memorial.[2] Then in addition to the taxes imposed in England, Virginia herself levied heavy export duties.[3]

It does not seem to me that the enumeration in itself was by any means the main cause of this decline in prices.[4] The duties were nearly all repaid on reëxportation,[5] and thus the only additional burden colonial tobacco labored under in the European markets, was the cost of the additional freight, since the ships would have to touch at English ports. But England, as Brougham has pointed out, was the natural *entrepôt* between the colonies and the countries North of Cape Finisterre.[6] And it is these countries which would especially want colonial tobacco,[7] Spain and Portugal obtaining their supply from the West Indies and Brazil. When we consider these facts we must say, that the enumeration in

---

[1] Gee (ed. 1731), p. 51.

[2] *The Case of the Planters of Tobacco* (London, 1733), pp. 4, 6.

[3] Ripley, *The Financial History of Virginia*, Columbia College Studies in History, Economics and Public Law, Vol IV, no. 1, pp. 57-62.

[4] Neill in *Virginia Carolorum*, p. 231, says that after the act of 1660 tobacco brought only a third of what it did before. He fails to consider the fact that in 1640, Virginia exported 1,300,000 lbs. of tobacco, and in 1688, 18,157,000 lbs. Likewise, he does not consider the heavy duties imposed by 12 Charles II., c. 4, nor the Virginia export duties.

[5] *Cf.* above.

[6] *An Inquiry into the Colonial Policy*, i, p. 246.

[7] See *Works* of D'Avenant, v, pp. 427, 428.

itself conduced but slightly to this decline in the prices. That it had a deleterious effect cannot be denied.[1]

The history of tobacco from 1700 to 1750 is most uneventful. The price seems to have remained approximately the same, occasionally rising and then again falling. Two and a half pence was the normal price paid per pound in Virginia.[2] The quantity exported from Virginia and Maryland increased gradually from about 28,000,000 pounds in 1700 to about 85,000,000 pounds in 1750.[3] Virginia exported usually somewhat more than half of the total quantity.[4] North Carolina produced a comparatively small amount of tobacco, and of this the larger part was shipped through Virginian ports.[5] The proportion of tobacco reexported from England to other countries was in 1700 about two-thirds, but it gradually increased to four-fifths of the quantity imported from the colonies.[6]

---

[1] Gee says, "if the Enumeration had been taken off, and our Merchants had had Liberty of sending that Tobacco, which is called Scrubs, and other ordinary Sorts directly to the Streights, the Crown might have saved that Money; for doubtless a great deal might be sold all along the Coast of Spain, within the Streights, as well as Leghorn, Coasts of Italy and Africa, and would beat out the Levant Tobacco, ours being much more valued," p. 51.

[2] Macpherson, iii, p. 163; *The Importance of the British Plantations in America to this Kingdom* (London, 1731), p. 73; *Dinwiddie Letters*, i, pp. 386, 386 n.; Brock, p. 224.

[3] Brock, p. 224; Burnaby's *Travels* (London, 1775), p. 21; p. 68.

[4] Brock, p. 222; *Dinwiddie Letters*, ii, p. 578; *New York Colonial Documents*, v, p. 606.

[5] Hawks, *History of North Carolina*, ii, p. 234, 236; *The Importance of the British Plantations in America*, pp. 70, 72. For some difficulties with Virginia about this, see Saunders, *The Colonial Records of North Carolina*, i, p. 628; Hening, iii, p. 253.

[6] The average importations into England from 1699 to 1709 amounted to 28,-858,666 lbs., and of this there were reexported 17,580,107 lbs. *Works* of Sir Charles D'Avenant (Whitworth ed., London, 1771), v, pp. 427, 428. *Cf.* also Brock, pp. 218, 222; Wood, *A Survey of Trade* (London, 1718), p. 144; Macpherson, iii, p. 264; Chalmers, *Revolt of the Colonies*, i, p. 218 n.; Carroll, *Historical Collections of South Carolina*, ii, p. 266; Adam Smith, *Wealth of Nations*, ii, p. 74; *New York Colonial Documents*, v, p. 619.

Of all colonial products tobacco was the most important. After the peace of Utrecht the amount of tobacco exported was equal in value to half of the total exports from the colonies to England.[1]   Its sole production determined the social and political constitution in Virginia.   It made the introduction of slavery most easy, and it made the county, and not the town, the unit of representation.[2]

§ 3. *Molasses and Rice.*   Molasses, the product of the British West India islands, was enumerated in Anne's reign.[3] Being a product of the West Indies, its history has only an indirect bearing on our subject, and this connection will be explained in a following chapter.   The history of the production of rice, which was enumerated at the same time, is, however, of vital importance.

About the time of the Revolution of 1688, by a lucky chance, the culture of rice was introduced into South Carolina.   A brigantine from Madagascar happening to stop at Carolina, the captain gave one of the residents a bag of seed-rice.[4]   Soil and climate being propitious, the cultivation quickly spread, and ultimately rice became the staple commodity of Carolina.   The rice produced was of excellent quality, contemporaries saying that it was the best in the world.[5]

Spain and Portugal used great quantities of rice, the demand for which, before Carolina produced it, Egypt and Lombardy had supplied.   When South Carolina began to

---

[1] *New York Colonial Documents*, v, p. 617.

[2] Howard, *Local Constitutional History of the United States*, i, p. 389.

[3] 3 and 4 Anne, c. 5, § xii.

[4] Anderson, iii, pp. 220, 221; Hewatt (Hewit. Hewat), *Historical Account of South Carolina and Georgia* (London, 1779), pp. 118–120; Drayton, *View of South Carolina* (Charleston, 1802), p. 115; Ramsay, *History of South Carolina*, ii, pp. 200–202; Carroll, *Historical Collection of South Carolina*, ii, p. 270; *The Importance of the British Plantations*, pp. 18, 19.

[5] Gee (1731), p. 21; J. Cary, *Discourse of Trade*, p. 52; Anderson, iii, p. 221.

produce rice, she entered into serious competition with these Eastern countries. American rice soon monopolized the Portuguese market and gained a foothold in Spain.[1] At this juncture one Captain Cole, moved by personal considerations, persuaded a member of parliament that the direct exportation of rice to Portugal was detrimental to English commerce.[2] Accordingly rice was enumerated.[3] Owing to the heavier freight charges, this increased the price by a third, and American rice gradually lost control of the Portuguese market. Only when the Egyptian and Italian crops failed was it imported by the Portuguese.[4]

To remedy this evil, a statute was passed in George II.'s reign. Rice was still kept an enumerated article,[5] but it could be sent direct from Carolina to any country south of Cape Finisterre.[6] Five years later Georgia rice obtained the same favor.[7] Immediately American rice regained control of its former market.[8]

---

[1] *New York Colonial Documents*, v, pp. 612, 613.

[2] Gee (ed. 1731), p. 21.   [3] 3 and 4 Ann., c. 5, § xii.

[4] Gee, p. 22. On an average from 1712–1717:

    28,073 cwts. of rice were imported into England from Carolina.

    2,478 cwts. of rice were reëxported to Portugal, Spain, etc.

    20,458 cwts. of rice were reëxported to countries N. of Finisterre.

    5,387 cwts. were kept for English consumption.

                       New York Colonial Documents, v, p. 613.

[5] 3 Geo. II., c. 28, § 1, confirmed the enumeration of rice. This statute did not take rice out of the enumerated commodities. It merely granted an especial privilege to rice from Carolina. *Cf. Historical Collections of South Carolina*, ii, p. 266.

[6] 3 Geo. II., c. 28, § ii. The clause in the statute is very ambiguous. I follow the interpretation John Ashley gives of 15 Geo. II., c. 33, § v, the wording of which is identical with this clause. *Considerations*, part ii. (London, 1741), p. 9.

[7] 8 Geo. II., c. 19. *Cf.* 20 Geo. II., c. 47; 27 Geo. II., c. 18. It was especially provided in these statutes that all rice so exported had to pay the half subsidy "which would have remained in case the said rice had been first imported into Great Britain and afterwards reëxported," 3 Geo. II., c. 28, § v.

[8] Anderson, iii, p. 463.

The quantity of rice exported increased rapidly. The whole export for the ten years ending in 1729 was 264,788 barrels; the exports for the following ten years amounted to 499,525 barrels, nearly double the former quantity.[1] In a good year Carolina exported 80,000 barrels; in the average year 50,000 barrels.[2]

Of this England consumed a very small quantity, about 2,000 to 3,000 barrels; that is, one-fifteenth to one-twenty-fifth of the total exports.[3] The countries south of Cape Finisterre used 10,000 barrels. Nearly all of these 10,000 barrels were sent to Portugal, for Spain used an inferior quality of rice that was produced in Turkey.[5] France did not allow the importation of foreign rice except under license.[4] Holland and Germany were the best markets, nearly three-fourths of all the rice exported being consumed there.[6]

[1] *Historical Collections of South Carolina*, i, p. 265. Ramsay, *History of South Carolina*, ii, p. 205. gives the following figures: 1724, 18,000 bls.; 1740, 91,110 bls.; 1754, 104,682 bls.; 1776, 142,000 bls. A barrel equals 500 lbs. *Historical Collections of South Carolina*, p. 202. Between March, 1730, and March, 1731, there sailed from Charleston 207 ships, carrying, besides other commodities, 41,957 bls. of rice, each barrel containing 500 lbs. *Force Tracts*, ii, "A Description of South Carolina," p. 6. In 1732 36,584 bls. of rice were exported from South Carolina. Anderson, iii, p. 463; Macpherson, iii, p. 198. In 1739 South Carolina exported 71,484 bls, and the next year 91,110 bls. Macpherson, iii, p. 222; p. 227.

[2] John Ashley, *Memorials and Considerations Concerning the Trade and Revenue of the British Colonies in America* (London, 1740,), Part i, p. 18.

[3] *Historical Collections of South Carolina*, ii, p. 266; Ashley, pt. i, p. 18.

The total quantity of rice exported from Carolina during ten years, 1730–1739, was sent to the following places:

Portugal	83,379 bls.
Gibraltar	958 bls.
Spain	3,570 bls.
France (1738–9)	9,500 bls.
Great Britain, Ireland, Plantations	30,000 bls.
Holland, Hamburg, Bremen	372,118 bls.

Historical Collections of South Carolina, p. 269.

[4] *Ibid.*, p. 267.   [5] *Ibid.*   [6] *Ibid.*, p. 267; Ashley, pt. i, p. 18.

The increase in the supply of rice did not cause a decline in its price; on the contrary, the price seems to have risen.[1] During the years 1745 to 1750 rice was worth forty-five shillings to fifty-five shillings a cwt. in Carolina currency, or six shillings five pence to eight shillings in sterling currency.[2] A few years before it was worth twelve shillings in Carolina currency.[3] The advance in price was not so rapid as these figures would seem to indicate. For as rice increased in value, its measure of value, the Carolina paper money, declined in value.

In the book of rates, rice was valued at one pound six pence eight shillings, the cwt. of one hundred and twelve pounds. Owing to the various subsidies and to the impost of 1692,[4] the duties were so increased as to amount in 1750 to about one hundred per cent. *ad valorem.* As little rice was consumed in England, and as nearly all the duty was repaid on reëxportation,[5] this heavy duty had little effect on the production of the article, and did not tend so much, as in the case of tobacco, to force the price down.

§ 4. *Naval Stores and Copper.* The policy of Louis XIV. involved England in frequent wars, and for success in these wars England had in the main to rely on her navy. As the navy grew and war followed war, the quantity of naval stores needed in England rapidly increased. Of these England could not produce a sufficient supply herself, but had to import them in ever-increasing quantities from foreign countries. Hemp, tar, pitch, masts, were imported from Denmark, Norway, Sweden and Russia. The balance of trade was against England, for these countries demanded money,

---

[1] For the value of the rice exported at the close of the war of the Spanish Succession, see *New York Colonial Documents*, v, p. 616.

[2] *Historical Collections of South Carolina*, ii, pp. 203, 234; Walker, *Money*, p. 326.   [3] *Ibid.*, p. 203.

[4] 4 and 5 W. and M., c. 5.   [5] Saxby, p. 215.

refusing to take England's manufactures in exchange. To the economist, as well as to the statesman, such a situation seemed full of peril. The one saw in this trade the gradual impoverishment of his country, the other the dependence of England for its naval supplies on countries with whom, at any time, it might become involved in war.[1]

The solution of the difficulty was to encourage the colonies to raise England's naval stores. Accordingly, at the time when molasses and rice were enumerated, bounties were offered on the production of naval stores. In order that the colonists might not send these commodities to foreign nations, they must be enumerated. Thus at the beginning of the war of the Spanish Succession, tar, pitch, turpentine, hemp, masts, yards, bowsprits were placed in the same category as tobacco and rice.[2]

Copper had been discovered in New York by the Dutch.[3] In nearly all the colonies copper mines existed, but in none of them was it produced to any great extent.[4] In 1715 we hear of a copper mine in New York, from which a ton of metal had been exported to Bristol.[5] Higginson, in 1700, wrote that there were copper mines in Massachusetts, "but for want of artists, there has been little got out of them."[6] In 1720 copper was very rare in New York,[7] while in New

---

[1] Gee, chap. xxix, p. 83, *et seq.*

[2] 3 and 4 Anne, c. 10, § viii. In the following chapter this subject will be treated in detail.

[3] *New York Colonial Documents*, i, p. 148; ii, pp. 29, 63.

[4] Bishop, *History of Manufactures*, pp. 471, 475, 483, 505, 507–510, 522, 524, 526, 532, 535, 541, 546, 548, 550, 551, 553, 555, 556, 574, 585, 586, 588, 599, 603, 610, 619. [5] *New York Colonial Documents*, v, 462.

[6] *Massachusetts Historical Society Collection*, 3d series, vii, p. 218. Bennett in 1740 speaks of copper mines in Massachusetts, but they are so far from water carriage, and the ore is so poor, that that they are not used. *Massachusetts Historical Society Proceedings*, 1860–62, p. 112.

[7] *New York Colonial Documents*, v, 556.

Jersey there was a little.[1]   On the discovery of what was deemed a very rich mine in New York,[2] copper in 1722 was enumerated.[3]   There were rumors of rich copper beds near Lake Superior as early as 1690,[4] and in 1770 we find the rumors repeated.[5]   The quantity produced remained always small, and the enumeration of this commodity was a measure of very slight importance.[6]

§ 5. *Beaver and other Furs.*   Washington Irving opens his charming work on Astoria with the following luminous paragraph: " Two leading objects of commercial gain have given birth to wide and daring enterprise in the early history of the Americas; the precious metals of the south, and the rich peltries of the north.   While the fiery and magnificent Spaniard, inflamed with the mania for gold, has extended his discoveries and conquests over those brilliant countries scorched by the ardent sun of the tropics, the adroit and buoyant Frenchman, and the cool and calculating Briton, have pursued the less splendid, but no less lucrative, traffic in furs amidst the hyperborean regions of the Cânadas, until they have advanced even within the Arctic circle."[7]   Parkman has frequently pointed out how important this trade was for New France.[8]   While this trade had such an all-pervad-

---

[1] *New York Colonial Documents*, v, 603.

[2] Macpherson, iii, p. 121; Anderson, iii, p. 371.   [3] 8 Geo. I., c. 18, § xxii.

[4] *New York Colonial Documents*, ix, p. 344.   [5] *Ibid.*, viii, pp. 92, 141.

[6] Burnaby, *Travels*, p. 16, mentions a copper mine upon the Roanoke, in Virginia.   [7] *Astoria*, p. 1.

[8] *Old Régime*, p. 302. " We come now to a trade far more important than all the rest together, one which absorbed the enterprise of the colony, drained the life-sap from other branches of commerce, and, even more than a vicious system of government, kept them in a state of chronic debility—the hardy, adventurous, lawless, fascinating fur trade. In the eighteenth century Canada exported a moderate quantity of timber, wheat, the herb called ginseng, and a few other commodities; but from first to last she lived chiefly on beaver-skins." *Cf.* pp. 303–315. See also Raynal's *Histoire Philosophique et Politique des deux Indes*, viii, p. 77.

ing influence on the growth and development of Canada, its influence on the colonies now constituting the United States was much less.

When the colonies were first founded the fur trade was of more importance than at any later time. Whether coming over with the desire for gain, or for the purpose of founding an ideal commonwealth, the commodity which the colonists obtained first in their traffic with the Indians, was fur.[1] But when after settlement, they began to develop the resources of the country, the fur trade declined in relative importance. Agriculture and the fisheries became the important industries of the Middle and Northern colonies. The fur most highly prized was the beaver. "Beaver was the one commodity in such constant demand that it served for a currency in all colonial trade," writes Weeden.[2] In 1634-5, it was ordered in Massachusetts that merchantable beaver be received at ten shillings the pound.[3]

As all the colonies had some traffic with the Indians, so all engaged in the fur trade, for fur was the only commodity the Indians had to sell.[4] In the Southern colonies, on account of the unfavorable climate, the trade was of less extent. Only in the North were the valuable furs, such as the beaver, found.[5]

[1] Roberts, *New York*, i, p. 22. Johnson, *Wonder-Working Providence* (ed. Poole), p. 16.

[2] Weeden, *Economic and Social History*, p. 96.

[3] *Colonial Records of Massachusetts*, i, p. 140. Beaver was used as a currency in New Netherlands, *New York Colonial Documents*, i, p. 386.

[4] *New York Colonial Documents*, i, p. 34, v, p. 549; Schuyler, *Colonial New York*, i, p. 136.

[5] *Historical Collections of South Carolina*, ii, p. 129. In 1731 it was said that the inhabitants of Carolina "carry on a great trade with the Indians, from whom they get these great Quantities of Deer Skins, and those of other Wild Beasts, in exchange for which they give them only Lead, Powder coarse cloth, Vermillion, Iron Ware, and some other Goods, by which they have a very considerable Profit."

By the very nature of things the Northern colonies were the centre of the fur trade. As the beaver skins were purchased from the Indians, this trade determined to an extent the attitude which the colonists should take towards them. Of all the Northern colonies, New York, on account of proximity to the Indians and its favorable geographical position, was most suited for this trade.[1] The Dutch, as early as 1616,[2] bought furs from the Indians, and in 1622 it was said that the trade was very profitable.[3] In 1656, 34,840 beaver skins were exported from Fort Orange and its vicinity.[4] When the settlements at Plymouth and Massachusetts were founded, the English sought a share of this lucrative commerce. But the Dutch, being on friendly terms with the Indians, and knowing their eagerness for rum and wampum, had great advantages over the English.[5] Yet at one time this trade was of vital importance to New England. As the English settlements extended the Indians were pushed back into New York, and the New Englander, to pursue this trade, was forced to go into the neighboring colony. This, as well as the profitable returns from fishing and agriculture, tended to decrease the fur trade in New England. Thus at the time when New York came into the possession of the English the French in Canada were the only serious rivals of the New Yorker in this trade.[6]

Between New France and New York the rivalry was intense. Already in 1666 we hear of a design of the French to engross all the beaver trade.[7] The Iroquois Indians were the inveterate enemies of the French, and the firm friends of

---

[1] *New York Colonial Documents*, v, p. 726.   [2] *Ibid.*, i, p. 14.

[3] *Ibid.*, i, p. 40; *cf.* Stone, *History of New York City*, pp. 40, 41.

[4] O'Callaghan, *History of New Netherlands*, ii, p. 310 n.

[5] Brodhead's *New York*, i, p. 171; Weeden, p. 38.

[6] Roberts, *New York*, p. 46; Weeden, p. 115.

[7] *New York Colonial Documents*, iii, p. 146.

the English.   This hostility naturally hampered the trade of
the French with the Iroquois, and it likewise prevented the
French from trading with the Indians who lived to the west-
ward of the Iroquois.[1]   The Jesuits sought to destroy this
advantage by converting the Iroquois to Catholicism, and
thereby estranging them from the heretical English.[2]   What
the Jesuits failed to do James II.'s Catholic policy accom-
plished.   Dongan, a Catholic, was appointed governor of
New York.   His object was to conciliate the French and to
make peace between them and the Iroquois.[3]   Whenever,
now, a quarrel arose between the Indians and the French,
the French said that they, joined by their English allies,
would destroy the Indians.   The Indians were thus alienated,
and despised the English "as a people depending on the
French."[4]

About this time a marked decline in the fur trade
of New York may be noticed.   Formerly New York sent
35,000 to 40,000 beaver skins to England.   In 1687
only 9,000 were sent.[5]   Continual complaints are made about
the loss of the fur trade.[6]   In 1696 a gentleman from Boston
writes that the French "are become in a manner sole masters of that trade, and will be continually encroaching, unless we put some stop thereunto."[7]   In 1700 it was said
that the beaver trade had sunk almost to nothing, only
15,241 skins having been exported the previous year.[8]

A little later, in 1722, beaver and other peltry were
enumerated.[9]   The colonists complained bitterly of this

---

[1] *New York Colonial Documents*, ix, p. 30 (1665).

[2] Parkman, *Old Régime*, pp. 316, 317.

[3] "Memoirs of Mr. Colden on the Fur Trade" in *New York Colonial Documents*, v, p. 731.

[4] *New York Colonial Documents*, v, p. 731.   [5] *Ibid.*, iii, p. 476.

[6] *Ibid.*, iv, pp. 2, 183.   [7] *Ibid.*, iv, p. 210.   [8] *Ibid.*, iv, p. 789.

[9] 8 Geo. I., c. 15, § xxiv.

restriction, saying that before the act they were able to export beaver to foreign countries.[1]   Yet on the other hand, at this time, the customs on beaver, payable in England, were considerably lessened.   By the book of rates of Charles II,[2] beaver skins were valued at six shillings eight pence, that is the duty imposed then at five per cent. was four pence a skin.   By the various subsidies and the impost of 1692, the duty at this time amounted to sixteen pence.   In 1722, beaver skins were rated at two shillings six pence,[3] that is the duty was now only six pence a skin.   While on the one hand beaver was enumerated, the duties payable in England were materially decreased.

The commodities sold to the Indians in exchange for beaver skins were wampum, blankets, trinkets, guns and ammunition.[4]   Most important, however, in this commerce was rum.   The Canadian exchanged brandy for furs, the Englishman obtained them in return for rum.[5]   And as the Indian drank only that he might get intoxicated, the pernicious effects of this trade on his morals can hardly be over-estimated.

Throughout the first half of the eighteenth century, the share of the English in the trade seems steadily to have declined.   In 1720, New York tried to regain the control of it from the French by prohibiting the selling of Indian goods to them.[6]   All efforts, however, proved unavailing. Colden in 1724 wrote, "that the French almost entirely engrossed the Fur Trade of America."[7]   Toward the end of the colonial period, the historian of New York, William

---

[1] *New York Colonial Documents*, v, p. 762.

[2] 12 Charles II., c. 4.   [3] 8 Geo. I., c. 15, § xiii.

[4] *Collections of the New York Historical Society*, 1st series, iv, p. 281; *New York Colonial Documents*, i, p. 150.

[5] *New York Colonial Documents*, vii, p. 613.

[6] *Ibid.*, v, p. 760; *cf.* pp. 779, 780.   [7] *Ibid.*, v, p. 729.

Smith, says that the fur trade was " very much impaired by the French wiles and encroachments."[1]

§ 6. *Sugar.* At first the Portuguese supplied all Europe with sugar obtained from their colony in Brazil.[2] From Brazil the cultivation of sugar was introduced into the English islands of Barbadoes[3] and Jamaica.[4] The English sugars, on account of their cheapness, soon gained control of the markets of Northern Europe, the Portuguese retaining only their trade with the Levant.[5] The low prices at which the English sold their sugar discouraged the Brazilians so that they entered into other lines of business, especially into mining. This gave the English a monopoly of the sugar trade with Northern Europe, and then they began to charge monopoly prices.[6] This advance in price in turn encouraged the French islands of the West Indies to produce more sugar,[7] and they soon became formidable rivals of the English.

In 1660 sugar was enumerated,[8] but at the same time the customs duties were so regulated as to give English sugar a practical monopoly of the home market.[9] From that time on we can see a gradual advance of the French colonies, and a growing jealousy of their prosperity on the part of the English.[10] As early as 1661 Barbadoes petitioned against

---

[1] *Collections of the New York Historical Society*, 1st series, iv, p. 280.

[2] Gee, p. 43.

[3] Schomburgk, *History of Barbadoes*, p. 142; Thomas, *An Historical Account of the West India Colonies* (London, 1690), p. 13.

[4] Long, *History of Jamaica* (London, 1774), i, p. 435.

[5] Gee, p. 43. Raynal, *Histoire des deux Indes*, vii, p. 314. "À cette époque (1660) les sucres anglais avaient remplacé le sucre portugais dans tout le nord de l'Europe. On peut croire qu'ils l'auraient également supplanté au midi , si l'obligation imposée aux navigateurs d'aborder dans les ports britanniques avant de passer le détroit de Gibraltar n'avait mis des obstacles insurmontables à ce commerce."

[6] *Ibid.*   [7] Gee, p. 44.   [8] 12 Charles II., c. 18.

[9] 12 Charles II., c. 4; Saxby, pp. 168, 169.

[10] This whole question will be more fully treated later on.

the enumeration of sugar.[1] Its growth, however, in the French colonies was checked by the restrictive policy that France adopted in the following years.[2] This enabled England till 1700 and later to retain control of the world's market.[3] But in 1717, France adopted a more liberal policy towards her colonies, with the result that, in 1740, the French sugars had driven the English out of the European markets.[4]

Against this loss the islands frequently petitioned, laying the blame on the enumeration of sugar.[5] In response to these continued complaints the "Molasses Act"[6] of 1733 was passed. This act laid prohibitory duties on sugar, rum and molasses imported from the foreign West Indies into the continental colonies. As this act was never executed, it afforded no relief. Some change had to be made in the enumeration. Therefore six years later a statute was[7] passed permitting the exportation of sugar to any European country South of Cape Finisterre in any vessel built in Great Britain and navigated according to law. The owners of such vessels must be Englishmen, of whom the major part resided in Great Britain, and the residue either in Great Britain or in any of the English sugar colonies in America. In

---

[1] Sainsbury's *Calendar*, 1661–1668, pp. 29, 30. In 1661 the French were called "an encroaching nation," *ibid.*, p. 168.

[2] Raynal, vii, pp. 11, 17; Clément, *Histoire de la Vie et de l'Administration de Colbert*, pp. 171, 172.

[3] J. Campbell, *Sugar Trade* (London, 1753), p. 10.

[4] Raynal, vii, p. 316. "Vers l'an 1740, le sucre des plantations françaises se trouva suffisant pour l'approvisionnement général; et, à cette époque, les Anglais se virent réduits à ne cultiver que pour leurs besoins." See *A Supplement* to Ashley's two books (London, 1744), pp. 4, 5; *The Present State of the British and French Trade to Africa and America* (London, 1745), pp. 8, 9.

[5] Ashley, part i, p. 1; p. 7.

[6] 6 Geo. II., c. 13.

[7] 12 Geo. II., c. 30.

order to prevent this trade from resulting in the clandestine importation of foreign goods into the colonies, it was also provided that within eight months after such ships had landed their cargoes of sugar they must touch in England. One provision of this act discriminated against New England merchants, who carried on a very large trade with the West Indies. This provision, requiring the major part of the owners to be residents of England, proved onerous,[1] and three years later the statute was amended so as to permit any of his majesty's subjects, in any English-built vessel, to carry sugar directly to the countries South of Cape Finisterre.[2] But these acts proved unavailing, and English sugar never again competed successfully with French sugar in the continental markets of Europe.

The loss of these markets was not so serious as at first sight it would seem. For during the seventeenth and eighteenth centuries the consumption of sugar in England had greatly increased.[3] Gee writes: " It is said before the War ten or twelve Millions of Pounds was as much as we spent at Home annually; but of late our Consumption hath been about sixty Millions of Pounds, and our Re-exportation scarcely one sixth Part of that."[4] In 1660, England consumed 1,000 hhds. of sugar, and exported 2,000 hhds. In 1700, England imported about 50,000 hhds., and exported about 18,000 hhds. In 1730, 100,000 hhds. were imported, and of this quantity only 18,000 hhds. were reëxported.[5]

[1] Ashley, part ii, p. 9.

[2] 15 Geo. II., c. 33, § v.

[3] Raynal, vii, p. 316. " . . . pour leurs besoins. Ils étaient encore très bornés au commencement du siècle; mais l'usage du thé et d'autres nouveaux goûts en ont prodigieusement augmenté la consommation."

[4] Gee, pp. 46, 47; cf. pp. 44, 45; p. 143.

[5] Campbell, Sugar Trade, p. 30.

In 1753, England imported 110,000 hhds., and reëxported scarcely any, only 6,000 hhds.[1]

While in the seventeenth century England consumed comparatively little sugar, in the eighteenth her demand for this commodity became very large.   At first most of the sugar imported from the West Indies was reëxported, but toward the middle of the eighteenth century the quantity thus sent to foreign markets became very insignificant.[2]   As the supply from the British West Indies increased, England's demand kept pace with it, and from the middle of the eighteenth century these islands seem never to have been able to produce much more sugar than was needed for consumption in the mother country.

Year.	Quantity of British Plantation Sugar Imported into England.	Quantity of Raw Sugar Exported from England.	Quantity of Refined Sugar Exported from England.
1699	427,573 cwts.	182,325 cwts.	14,302 cwts.
1700	489,326 cwts.	165,391 cwts.	17,644 cwts.
1705	370,157 cwts.	71,822 cwts.	690 cwts.
1710	507,662 cwts.	117,075 cwts.	2,146 cwts.
1715	617,414 cwts.	143,337 cwts.	4,481 cwts.
1720	706,385 cwts.	121,778 cwts.	3,106 cwts.
1725	851,952 cwts.	147,408 cwts.	6,293 cwts.
1730	1,024,078 cwts.	167,980 cwts.	14,538 cwts.
1735	903,634 cwts.	69,899 cwts.	21,070 cwts.
1740	706,947 cwts.	67,144 cwts.	15,046 cwts.
1745	655,199 cwts.	78,344 cwts.	17,689 cwts.
1750	915,344 cwts.	107,964 cwts.	21,846 cwts.
1755	1,202,679 cwts.	110,853 cwts.	14,364 cwts.
1760	1,374,720 cwts.	143,683 cwts.	58,650 cwts.
1765	1,227,159 cwts.	149,125 cwts.	114,851 cwts.
1770	1,818,229 cwts.	199,738 cwts.	43,609 cwts.

Compiled from Edwards, *History of West Indies* (London, 1793), ii. pp. 498, 499. *Cf.* also Macpherson, iii. p. 200; p. 263; Raynal, vii., p. 446; Ashley, part ii., p. 29; *New York Colonial Documents*, v, p. 619.

[2] Campbell's *Sugar Trade*, p. 30.

CHAPTER IV. THE RESTRICTIONS ON COLONIAL MANUFACTURES.

§ 1. *The Economic and Political Principles.* According to the mercantile system the economic condition of a nation was judged by its balance of trade. Thus the aim of the statesmen of the seventeenth and eighteenth centuries was to secure for their nations as favorable a balance of trade as possible. One way in which to accomplish this result was to increase the exportation of manufactured goods; and it was in this connection that colonies were regarded as especially useful. While they were to be the source of England's raw materials, it was desired that they should at the same time become an important factor in the consumption of its manufactures. To use a phrase common in those days, they were to be the vent of England's manufactures. Thus, in 1663, Fortrey writes, " I conceive no forein Plantation should be undertaken, or prosecuted, but in such countreys, that may increase the wealth and trade of this nation, either in furnishing us, with what we are otherwise forced to purchase from strangers, or else by increasing such commodities, as are vendible abroad; which may both increase our shipping, and profitably employ our people." [1]

If the colonies were allowed to enter upon manufactures, the good results obtained by enumerating the raw materials would be lost. For if the colonies had their own manufac-

[1] *England's Interest*, pp. 34, 35. J. Thorold Rogers writes, "the doctrine that the commercial prosperity of a country depends on the creation, maintenance, and extension of a sole market for its products and for its supplies, was prevalent from the discovery of the New World and the Cape Passage down to the war of American Independence." *Economic Interpretation of History*, p. 323.

tures less attention would be given to raising the raw materials, and those that were raised would be consumed at home. The colonies would cease to import manufactures from England, and might even export their own to foreign markets and there compete with English manufactures. These possible events would tend to create an unfavorable balance of trade for England, for if they manufactured for themselves the colonists would gradually cease to import from England: they might also begin to export to foreign countries, and thereby encroach on the markets for English exports. Moreover, if the enumerated commodities should be produced in smaller quantities the English manufacturer would have to pay more for his raw materials. The cost of his manufactured articles would thus be increased, less would be exported, and that little would have to compete with goods produced, in all probability, under much more favorable circumstances. Perhaps England might even have to import her raw materials from foreign countries, and pay for the same in money. Thus we can see that the laying of restrictions on colonial manufactures was a necessary consequence of the mercantile system. Furthermore, the policy of enumeration would be incomplete without such restriction or prohibition. If one measure in the policy were omitted, the other would be rendered nugatory.

Having thus outlined the main currents of thought, it may be well to illustrate them by a few extracts from the writings of contemporaries. They will clearly show the jealous spirit with which England watched every sign of the development of manufactures in the colonies. In 1705 Lord Cornbury wrote, the colonists have entered " upon a Trade which I am sure *will hurt England in a little time;* for I am well informed that upon Long-Island and Connecticut, they are setting up a Woollen Manufacture, and I myself have seen Serge made upon Long Island that any man may wear." [1] Gee

[1] O'Callaghan, *Documentary History of New York*, i, p. 713.

writes, "now as it is plain, keeping the Planters to the raising of Materials in the Plantations is the certain Way to en-
rich them, it is proper, for creating a right Understanding
and true Friendship between the Planters in the Colonies,
and for making the Government as well as the Manufacturers
here easy, to come into the same Measures that other Nations
have done who have Plantations abroad." For "great Care
has been taken to prevent their natural born Subjects from
going upon such Manufactures as did interfere with theirs at
home."[1] A writer in 1770 shows clearly the attitude of
England toward colonial manufactures. "The greatest and
most general fear, and, indeed, what the colonies of late seem
to threaten us with," he writes, "is their going into manufactures, and thereby supplying themselves with what they
now take from us. If this was likely to happen, the vigilance
of our legislature would doubtless take measures to prevent
it. . . . Nothing, certainly, would create greater heart-burn-
ings and discontent in Great Britain than her colonies going
into manufactures."[2]

In addition to these purely economic reasons for restricting manufactures, there were others that appealed especially
to statesmen. The statesmen of England recognized that
economic independence precedes political independence and
is, in a measure, the cause of it. They feared that if the
colonies were to learn to manufacture their essential commodities, they would gradually become estranged from the
mother country and might ultimately attain political independence. Thus Lord Cornbury says, "I declare my opinion to be that all these Colloneys, which are but twigs
belonging to the Main Tree (England), ought to be kept

[1] Gee, pp. 76, 77.

[2] *Essay on Trade and Commerce*, by J. Cunningham (?) Lond. 1770, pp. 194, 197, quoted in O. L. Elliott's *The Tariff Controversy*, p. 9. (Leland Stanford Jr. University Monographs.]

entirely dependant upon & subservient to England, and that can never be if they are suffered to goe on in the notions they have, that as they are Englishmen, soe they may set up the same manufactures here as people may do in England; for the consequence will be that if once they can see they can cloath themselves, not only comfortably but handsomely too, without the help of England, they who are already not very fond of submitting to Government would soon think of putting in Execution designs they had long harbourd in their breasts. This will not seem strange when you consider what sort of people this Country is inhabited by."[1]

The opposition of England to colonial manufactures is well shown by an incident related by Franklin. The distinguished philosopher had drawn up a plan for conciliating England and the colonies, and in this plan there was a proposition that "all the acts restraining manufactures in the colonies" be repealed.[2] Strong objections were made to this proposition, on the ground "that restraining manufactures in the colonies was a favorite idea here (England); and, therefore, they wished that article to be omitted, as the proposing it would alarm and hinder perhaps the considering and granting others of more importance."[3]

In the eyes of England the whole colonial system would be overturned, were the colonies to manufacture their own supplies. What Bancroft so forcibly and so graphically says, is hardly an exaggeration: "To manufacture like Englishmen was esteemed a sort of forgery, punishable, like an imitation of the British coin."[4] A close watch was, there-

---

[1] O'Callaghan, *Documentary History of New York*, i, p. 712; *cf.* Townshend's *Remarks* (Lond., 1760), p. 50, "and as they increase daily in People and in Industry, the Necessity of a Connection with England, with which they have no natural Intercourse by a Reciprocation of Wants, will continually diminish."

[2] Franklin, *Works* (ed. Sparks), v, p. 13.   [3] *Ibid.*, p. 17.

[4] *History* (Boston, 1876), ii, p. 520.

fore, kept on colonial industry. Governors were instructed to discourage all manufactures and to give accurate accounts of any indications of the same. Thus, when manufactures had once been started in the colonies, it is not strange, in view of the prevalent feeling in England, that they were vigorously repressed.

In the following sections we shall show how in the Southern colonies no manufactures existed, and we shall attempt to account for the early rise of manufactures in New York and in New England.[1]

§ 2. *Absence of Manufactures in the Southern Colonies.* All attempts[2] to make the Virginians abandon the cultivation of tobacco for manufacturing proved futile. The raising of tobacco always remained their principal occupation.[3] It was for the economic advantage of Virginia to produce tobacco, to sell it in England, and out of its proceeds to buy English manufactures. Thus it is by no means strange that the Virginians imported all their manufactures from England. Beverley in a celebrated passage writes, " they have their clothing of all sorts from England, as linen, woolen and silk, hats and leather. The very furs that their hats are made of perhaps go first from thence. Nay they are such abominable ill-husbands, that tho' their country be over-run with wood, yet they have all their wooden ware from England; their cabinets, chairs, tables, stools, chests, boxes, cart-wheels and all other things, even so much as their bowls and birchen brooms, to the eternal reproach of their laziness." [4] Virginia

---

[1] " It is observable that there are more trades carried on, and manufactures set up in the provinces on the continent of America to the northward of Virginia, prejudicial to the trade and manufactures of Great Britain, particularly in New England, than in any other of the British colonies." Macpherson, iii, p. 190.

[2] Hening, iii, pp. 120, 121, 124, 242, 272, 287, 503, 504, 505; Beverley, iv, pp. 58, 63, 93, 94.

[3] *Massachusetts Historical Society Collections,* 3d series, vii, p. 232.

[4] Beverley, iv, p. 58.

seems not to have had an artisan class. There were few or none who could make such common articles as shoes or chairs. All was imported from England.[1] Even the wood used for building houses, was sent to England, and when dressed and cut there, was sent back to Virginia for use.[2] During the entire colonial period Virginia retained this characteristic.[3] Shortly before the Revolution Jefferson wrote as follows about Virginia: "And such is our attachment to agriculture, and such our preference for foreign manufactures, that be it wise or unwise, our people will certainly return, as soon as they can, to the raising raw materials, and exchanging them for finer manufactures than they are able to execute themselves."[4] "Carpenters, masons, smiths, are wanting in husbandry; but for the general operations of manufactures, let our workshop remain in Europe."[5]

Like Virginia,[6] Maryland paid for the manufactures she consumed by exporting tobacco to England. In regard to manufactures her situation was identical with that of Virginia. In 1721 it was said of Maryland, "the Inhabitants wear the like Cloathing, & have the same furniture within their houses with those in this Kingdom [England]. The

---

[1] "The Tobacco Plantations take from England their Cloathing, Houshould Goods, Iron Manufactures of all Sorts, Saddles, Bridles, Brass and Copper Wares; and notwithstanding their dwelling among the Woods, they take their very Turners wares, and almost every thing else that may be called the Manufacture of England." Gee, pp. 20, 21.

[2] Palmer, *Calendar of Virginia State Papers*, i, p. lv.

[3] *Dinwiddie Papers*, i, p. 385.

[4] *Writings* of Jefferson (Wash., 1854), viii, p. 405.

[5] *Ibid.*, p. 406. Burnaby's *Travels*. pp. 21, 22: "Their manufactures are very inconsiderable. They make a kind of cotton-cloth, which they clothe themselves with in common, and call after the name of their country; and some inconsiderable quantities of linen, hose, and other trifling articles: but nothing to deserve attention."

[6] *Cf.* Lodge, *A Short History of the English Colonies in America*, pp. 62, 63.

Slaves are cloathed with Cottons, Kerseys, flannel, & coarse linens, all imported."[1]

What tobacco was to Maryland and Virginia, rice was to South Carolina. With this commodity all the manufactured goods used in the colony were bought in England. Since artisans were so scarce, most of the shoes came from England. There was no potter, it was said at one time, in the whole colony, and all the glass and earthen-ware which was used had to be imported.[2] As in the case of Maryland and Virginia, all manufactured articles[3] were imported. North Carolina was likewise characterized by this total absence of manufactures.[4]

In the Southern colonies thus there was a marked absence of manufacturing even in its most rudimentary forms.[5] The reason was that a unit of labor spent in agriculture proved far more renumerative than the same unit devoted to manufactures. Many circumstances conduced to bring about this result. Their staple products, rice and tobacco, not being extensively produced in Europe, found a ready market there;

[1] *New York Colonial Documents*, v, p. 606. See Lodge, p. 117.

[2] Force, *Tracts*, ii, " A Description of South Carolina," pp. 7, 8; *Historical Collections of South Carolina*, ii, p. 131.

[3] *Historical Collection of South Carolina*, ii, p. 254. The following commodities were imported from England into South Carolina: "All sorts of Woollen Cloths, Stuffs, and Druggetts; Linens, Hollands, Printed Calicoes and Linens; Silks and Muslins; Nails of all sizes, Hoes, Hatchetts, and all Kinds of Iron-wares; Bedticks, Strong Beer, Bottled Cider, Raisins, Fine Earthen wares, Pipes, Paper, Rugs, Blankets, Quilts, Hats from 28 to 12 s. piece; Stockings from 1 to 8 sh. piece; Gloves; Pewter Dishes and Plates; Brass and Copper wares; Guns, Powder, Bulletts, Flints, Glass Beads, Cordage, Woollen and Cotton Cards, Steel Hand mills, Grind-stones; Looking and Drinking Glasses; Lace, Thread coarse and fine; Mohair, and all Kinds of Trimmings for Cloaths, Pins, Needles, &c;" *cf.* also *ibid.*, pp. 229–231.

[4] Hawks, *North Carolina*, pp. 239, 240; Lodge, p. 153.

[5] " In that part of the United States situated to the South of Pennsylvania there are no manufactures whatsoever." W. C. Ford, *Report of 1791*, p. 29.

while in the colonies themselves the network of rivers made the transportation of these products most easy. Thus economically the most profitable employment of the Southern colonies was agriculture.

§ 3. *The Early Rise of Manufactures in the Northern Colonies.* Another problem now confronts us, namely, to account for the early rise of manufactures in the Northern colonies. The chief pursuit of a young settlement is agriculture. There land is cheap, while labor is dear.[1] Nor is it in accord with psychological principles that a man should be willing to work for wages, when for the asking he can have land and become his own master. Thus a contemporary, Johnson, writes, "and for cloth, here is and would be materials enough to make it; but the Farmers deem it better for their profit to put away their cattel and corn for cloathing, then to set upon making of cloth."[2] We should expect to find wheat and grain produced in the Northern colonies, and that these colonies would become the granary of old England. About 1640, in Massachusetts, signs of such a course of development appear. At that time the staple commodities of the colony were wheat, oats, peas, barley, beef, pork, fish, butter, cheese, timber, tar, and boards. With these the people of Massachusetts, says Johnson, "not only fed their Elder Sisters, Virginia, Barbados, and many of the Summer Islands that were prefer'd before her fruitfulness, *but also the Granamother of us all, even the firtil Isle of Great Britain.*"[3] Before, however, the exports to England became large, the trade was checked by the policy of the mother country. The change came in 1660.

With the Restoration begins the supremacy of the landed

[1] Johnson, *Wonder-Working Providence* [Ed. Poole], p. 207; *New York Colonial Documents*, v, p. 598.

[2] Johnson, *Wonder-Working Providence*, p. 174.   [3] *Ibid.*, p. 208.

classes in England. In that year the remnants of the feudal
dues were commuted into an excise falling chiefly on the
landless and the urban population.[1] By a statute of this
year, and by others enacted later in the reign of Charles II.,
prohibitory customs duties were levied on agricultural products, such as rye, barley, peas, beans, oats, and wheat.[2]
These were the earliest Corn Laws.[3] Likewise during this
reign the importation of salt provisions, including beef, pork,
bacon,[4] and butter[5] from the colonies was absolutely prohibited. In addition, the whale-fisheries of New England
were discouraged by the levy of discriminating duties on oil
and blubber caught, and imported into England in colonial
shipping.[6] But it was with the commodities affected by
these acts, that New England would most naturally buy her
manufactured goods from England.

This feature of England's policy during the Restoration
had thus two effects. On the one hand, it rendered a middle
market necessary for the Northern colonies; on the other, it
made these colonies much more independent of the mother
country as regards manufactures. Both of these results were
not in accord with the normal economic development of the
colonies, as regulated by the laws of trade. For if the
colonists exported these staple commodities to other countries, they found their profits diminished from the fact that
no manufactures could be taken directly back on the return
voyage. The vessel had either to return empty, or to make
a roundabout trip and load in England. The effect of England's policy was, through a restriction of the market, to
render the production of these staple commodities less profit-

---

[1] Hallam, *Constitutional History of England*, ii, pp. 298–300.

[2] Saxby, pp. 111–114.

[3] The first Corn Law was enacted in the reign of Edward IV. *Cf.* Faber, *Die Enststehung des Agrarschutzes*, p. 85.

[4] 18 Charles II., c. 2.   [5] 30 Charles II., c. 2, § ix.   [6] 25 Charles II., c. 7.

able. Thus New England, and later the Middle colonies, not being allowed to exchange their normal products for England's manufactures, were forced to begin manufacturing for themselves. And that this was the ultimate cause for the early rise of manufactures can be shown by a few extracts from letters and reports of those days.

In 1705, Lord Cornbury ascribed the rise of manufactures in New York to "the want wherewithall to make returns for England."[1] A little later, in 1721, clearer expression was given to the problem in Massachusetts. " It is, therefore, to be presumed," the report says, "that necessity, and not choice, has put them upon erecting manufactures; not having sufficient commodities of their own to give in exchange for those they do receive already from Great Britain."[2] Paul Dockminique's report of 1732 says, "they have no staple commodities of their own growth to exchange for our manufactures; which puts them under greater necessity, as well as under greater temptation of providing for themselves at home."[3] In 1764 Colden spoke of New York as a colony consuming a vast quantity of manufactures of Great Britain, though it produced no staple that could be exported directly thither.[4]

That this is the true explanation can be seen from what took place in Virginia during the War of the Spanish Succession. During this war the price of tobacco fell, and tobacco was at the same time over-produced. The Virginians, having nothing with which to make returns to England, were forced to manufacture coarse cloth for themselves.[5]

---

[1] *New York Colonial Documents*, iv, pp. 1150, 1151; *Documentary History of New York*, i, p. 711.

[2] *New York Colonial Documents*, v, p. 598. cf. Gee, p. 102; p. 24.

[3] Macpherson, iii, p. 190.   [4] *New York Colonial Documents*, vii, p. 612.

[5] *Spotswood Letters*, i, p. 71. See also Postlethwayt, *Savary's Universal Dictionary of Trade and Commerce*, i, p. 533; *Parliamentary History*, xvi, pp. 159, 160.

Thus this interference with the normal market for the staple products of the colonies was the cause of the early development of manufacturing in New England and New York. But if this was the fundamental cause, it was by no means the sole one. Other elements conduced, though in a less degree, to the same result. Even without the Corn Laws, it is probable that there would have been more artisans and much more rudimentary manufacturing in New England than in Virginia. For the New Englander was by nature drawn to such pursuits, both from his origin and his intimate contact with Dutch civilization. Many of the later immigrants also were artisans. The Scotch-Irish, fugitives from the harsh laws of England, were skilled in the textile industries, and we hear of them setting up linen manufactures in New England.[1] We likewise find Huguenots engaged in manufacturing.[2] When the fugitives from the Palatinate came to America, fears were expressed that they would enter upon these pursuits.[3] In New York it was ordered that a clause be introduced into every grant of land to them, declaring it void if the grantee entered upon the manufacture of woolens or other goods.[4]

There were other and more special causes which contributed to the rise of certain industries in the North. The cheapness of beaver and its plentiful supply led to the rapid development of the hat industry. The vast stores of lumber made ship-building in New England profitable. Manufactures were also encouraged by law;[5] but it is significant that the legal encouragements offered by Virginia were not strong enough to overcome the natural obstacles.

[1] *New York Colonial Documents*, v, p. 598; Burnaby's *Travels*, p. 82; *Proceedings of the Massachusetts Historical Society*, 1860–1862, p. 111.

[2] Baird, *The Huguenots in America*, ii, p. 217.

[3] *New York Colonial Documents*, v, p. 88.   [4] *Ibid.*, p. 118.

[5] *Colonial Records of Massachusetts*, i, pp. 294, 303.

It thus appears that the fundamental cause of the early rise of manufacturing in the Northern colonies was that the importation of their staple products into England was prohibited either absolutely or by heavy duties. They were consequently left without adequate means of payment; a balance of trade naturally unfavorable to them was made increasingly so by the policy of England.

§ 4. *The Restrictions on the Manufacture of Woolens.* In view of the importance of the woolen industry from the days of Edward III.,[1] it is not strange that English statesmen should have early devoted their attention to the restricting of this branch of production in the colonies. Toward the end of the seventeenth century a statute was passed—which likewise introduced the policy of crushing out the Irish woolen industry—providing that no woolen manufactures should be exported from the colonies, or transported from one colony to another, or conveyed from one place to another in the same colony.[2] This statute did not forbid the making of woolen fabrics for private consumption, but simply forbade the making of woolens for the public market. At this time the woolens exported from England had to pay heavy duties. The next year, however, these duties were abolished and the exportation of woolens from England was made free.[3] It will be proper now to inquire how far this law was obeyed, and to what extent the industry which it was intended to check, actually progressed in the colonies.

From Lord Cornbury we learn that in 1705 Long Island

---

[1] W. J. Ashley, "The Early History of the English Woollen Industry," *Publications of the American Economic Association*, vol. ii, no. 4, pp. 1–3; W. Longman, *Life and Times of Edward III.*, i, pp. 3, 85.

[2] 10 and 11 Will. III., c. 10, § xix. "Wool, woollfells, shortlings, mortlings, woollstocks, worsted, bay, woollen yarn, cloth, serge, bays, kerseys, says, frizes, druggets, cloth-serges, shalloons, drapery stuff, or any woolen manufacture."

[3] 11 and 12 Will. III., c. 20.

and Connecticut produced excellent serges.[1]　In 1708 Mr. Caleb Heathcote wrote of New York, "they are already so far advanced in their Manufactoryes that ¾ of ye linen and Woolen they use, is made amongst 'em—espetially the courser sort."[2]　In the same year Lord Cornbury wrote as follows to the Board of Trade: "The Manufactures settled here in this Province are Linnen and Woollen; they make very good Linnen for common use, and I do'nt doubt but in time they will improve that considerably; as for the woollen I think they have brought that too great perfection already."[3]

In answer to these accounts the Lords of Trade, in 1715, ordered Governor Hunter to give all possible legal discouragements to these undertakings.[4]　Commenting on these orders, Governor Hunter said: "The people of this Town and Albany, which make a great part of the Province, wear no cloathing of their own manufacture, but if the letters mentioned in your Lordships mean the planters and poorer sort of country people, the computatn is rather less than more."　And he adds, "neither does it consist with my knowledge that ever any home spun was sold in the shops."[5]　In 1721 a similar statement was made.[6]　President Van Dam in 1731 wrote to Secretary Popple, "I do not know of any Laws made here or any Manufactures set up that may affect the Manufactures of Great Britain."[7]

In 1749, Clinton said that the people of New York make

---

[1] *Documentary History of New York*, i, p. 711; *New York Colonial Documents*, iv, pp. 1150, 1151.

[2] *Documentary History of New York*, i, p. 712; *New York Colonial Documents*, v, p. 63.

[3] *Ibid.*, v, p. 59.　　　　[4] *Ibid.*, v, pp. 413, 414.

[5] *Ibid.*, v, p. 460; *Documentary History of New York*, i, pp. 713, 714.

[6] *New York Colonial Documents*, v, p. 556.　　　[7] *Ibid.*, v, p. 925.

homespun, to supply themselves somewhat with the necessaries of clothing.[1] Burnaby, who traveled through the
colonies in 1759 and 1760, says that New York made "a
small quantity of cloth."[2] Finally in 1765, Mr. Colden
wrote: "What has been published of the Manufactures lately
set up, are absolute Falsehoods, and yet they are not
ashamed to publish them where they are known to be such.
All the wool in America is not sufficient to make Stockens
for the Inhabitants, and the severe Winters in North
America, render the production of Wool in great quantities
impracticable."[3]

In New Jersey,[4] Burnaby says there were no manufactures
worth mentioning, but in Pennsylvania many stockings were
manufactured, and "some woollens have also been fabricated,
but not . . . to any amount."[5] The woolen manufacture in the Middle colonies, did not extend beyond the production of what was used in the family.[6]

The condition of this industry in New England was
similar. Coarse cottons and woolens were made for the use
of the lower classes of society.[7] Thus we are told that
Massachusetts, in 1721, made "all sorts of common Manufactures," "coarse Cloths, druggets & serges," used, however, by only the "meanest sort of people."[8] Forty years
later Burnaby writes about the same commonwealth, "like
the rest of the colonies they also endeavor to make woollens,
but have not yet been able to bring them to any degree of
perfection; indeed it is an article in which I think they will

[1] *New York Colonial Documents*, vi, p. 511. [2] *Travels*, p. 110.

[3] *New York Colonial Documents*, vii, pp. 799, 800.

[4] *Travels*, p. 123. [5] *Ibid.*, p. 82. See Lodge, pp. 229, 230.

[6] *Documentary History of New York*, i, p. 722; iv, pp. 182, 183; *New York Colonial Documents*, v, p. 938.

[7] Chalmers, *Revolt*, ii, p. 12. [8] *New York Colonial Documents*, v, p. 597.

not easily succeed."[1]   In Rhode Island there were no important manufactures,[2] and in Connecticut "coarse linens and woollens for the poorer sort of people" were made.[3]

In a small pamphlet, concerning the state of New England, written in 1689, we read, that "some Manufactures there are amongst them, but not a Twentieth part of what the Country hath need of, or is consumed there, most of their Cloathing as to Woollen and Linnen, all sorts of Upholstery Wares, Haberdashers and Silk Wares, Stuffs, Silks, etc., they had from England."[4]   In 1740, the historian Bennett wrote as follows about the New Englanders: "They send to England in return for almost all sorts of English goods, but more especially clothing for men, women, and children.   They have paper manufactured here, and some coarse woollen cloths; but workmen's wages are so high in this part of the World, that they find it cheaper to import them from London."[5]

In the latter half of the seventeenth century the Northern colonies, as a result of England's policy, were forced to begin the manufacture of woolens.   So serious did these attempts seem, that England restricted the growth of this industry.   As a result of restriction, and of the increase in demand for their staple commodities by the West Indies, the woolen industry in the colonies never passed out of the embryonic stage.   The Northern colonies were essentially agricultural and fishing communities.   On each farm there was a certain number of sheep, from which the farmer obtained his wool.   During the severe winter months, when out-of-door labor was at a stand-still, the servants were employed

[1] *Travels*, p. 137.   [2] *Ibid.*, p. 101.

[3] *Massachusetts Historical Society Collection*, 2nd Series, p. 218.

[4] *Force Tracts*, iv, "A Brief Relation," p. 8; *cf.* Macpherson, iii, p. 189.

[5] *Proceedings of Massachusetts Historical Society*, 1860–1862, p. 111.

n weaving this wool into home-spun, for the use of the household.[1]   Itinerant weavers traveled about the country putting the finishing touches on these fabrics.[2]   The woolens, which were made, were used chiefly by the great body of people, while the merchants, the inhabitants of the cities, all whose occupations were not agricultural, used woolens imported from England.[3]   In general the act of parliament was well obeyed,[4] since it carried no hardship with it in the eighteenth century.   The amount of woolens exported from England to the colonies was very great.[5]   On an average, about 1717, England exported to the colonies woolens to the value of £147,438, while at the same time the exports of iron manufactures amounted to only £35,631.   The amount of woolens exported was equal in value to one half of the total exports of British manufactures from England to the colonies.[6]

§ 5. *The Manufacture of Hats.*   As mentioned above, the commodity which the colonists obtained from their commercial intercourse with the Indians was mainly beaver.   In addition to being sent to England to pay for manufactures, this beaver was made into hats in the colonies.[7]   In 1721 there were some hatters in Massachusetts.[8]   And in 1732 Governor Cosby of New York wrote that "the hatt makeing

---

[1] Macpherson, iii, p. 187; Bishop, i, p. 339.

[2] *Documentary History of New York*, i, p. 734.

[3] *Cf.* Report of 1731/2 in *Macpherson*, iii, p. 187; Bishop, i, p. 339.

[4] A petition of 1769 from Massachusetts says, " their clothing, of which in that cold climate more is required than otherwise would be necessary, and which, some small part made by themselves only excepted, is made of the woollens and other manufactures of Great Britain." *Parliamentary History*, xvi, p. 482.

[5] Sir William Keith, *A Collection of Papers and other Tracts* (London, 1749), p. 171.

[6] *New York Colonial Documents*, v, p. 617.

[7] *Ibid*, iv, p. 572; v, p. 774; vi, p. 511.   [8] *Ibid.*, v, p. 598.

trade here seemed to promise to make the greatest advance to the prejudice of Great Brittain."[1]

Quite a considerable industry seems to have sprung up. Hats were exported even to foreign markets, such as Spain, Portugal and the West Indies.[2] In 1731 the Company of Feltmakers petitioned Parliament to prohibit the exportation of hats from the American colonies, representing that foreign markets were supplied thence and that some were even exported to England. The committee, reporting on this petition, said that in New York and New England, ten thousand beaver hats were annually manufactured.[3] In consequence of this petition a statute was passed.[4]

Since the colonists formerly bought hats from England, where "the art and mystery" of making hats was very perfect, and since now these colonies made their own hats and competed in foreign markets with England, it was provided:

I. That after 1732 no hats should be put on board a ship or a cart for exportation to Europe or to England, or for transportation from one plantation to another.

II. That no one should make felts or hats but such as had served an apprenticeship. Nor could a journeyman be employed, unless he had served his apprenticeship for seven years. No master should have more than two apprentices and these could not serve for less than seven years, nor could they be negroes. These provisions were copied from the celebrated "Apprenticeship Law" of Elizabeth.

This act does not seem to have been very strictly executed. Bennett says, in 1740, "there are a good many hatters, too, in New England, but they are chiefly employed in making up beaver-hats, which are sold cheaper here than in

---

[1] *New York Colonial Documents*, v, p. 938.

[2] Macpherson, iii, pp. 189, 190; Anderson, iii, p. 440; Weeden, p. 504.

[3] Bishop, i, p. 342.   [4] 5 Geo. II., c. 22.

England: but the coarse hats they import from London, which comes much cheaper to the hatters than they can make them."[1]   Burnaby mentions the fact that in 1759 Pennsylvania made better beaver hats than are made in Europe.[2]   The industry must, however, by its very nature, have always remained comparatively unimportant.

§ 6. *The Iron Industry and Its Regulations.*   The production of iron ranked third in importance among English industries.   In 1719 it employed 200,000 people.   The English iron mines could not supply the vast demands, nor could the forests, gradually becoming thinner since the days of Henry VIII., afford sufficient fuel.   In the third decade of the eighteenth century, about 20,000 tons of iron were annually imported, of which three-quarters came from Sweden.[3]   The price was from £10 to £12 per ton, and since nearly all was paid for in metal, from £200,000 to £240,000 were yearly taken from England.   In addition, fuel to the value of £200,000 was annually imported.[4]   Such a situation seemed to the economists of those days not only precarious but calamitous.   The solution of the difficulty, as Joshua Gee suggested, would be to get iron from the American colonies.[5]

[1] *Proceedings of the Massachusetts Historical Society*, 1860–62, p. 111.

[2] *Travels*, p. 82.

. [3] Macpherson, iii, p. 73, p. 214; Anderson, iii, p. 319; *cf.* Gee, pp. 160, 161, "I had lately seen an account of the whole Quantity of Iron exported from Stockholm and Gottenburg to the several Parts of Europe, in the Year 1729; whereby it appears, that there was ship'd for Great Britain and Ireland, from those two Ports only, (besides what we had from Spain, Norway and Russia), above 19,000 Tons.'

[4] *Ibid.; cf. A Letter to a Member of Parliament Concerning the Naval Store-Bill* (Lond., 1720), p. 10.   *Cf.* Gee, pp. 16, 17, p. 121; Scrivenor, *History of the Iron Trade*, p. 70.

[5] "The making and supplying ourselves with Pig and Bar Iron from the Colonies, is also very material, since Foreigners draw between two and three hundred thousand Pounds *per annum* from us for that Commodity, and all to a Trifle in ready Money."   Gee, p. 68.

All the colonies from Massachusetts to Carolina contained iron. In Maryland and Virginia there were rich iron mines, while in the North bog iron was obtained from the ferruginous sediment of the marshy lands. Early in the history of Virginia we hear of an iron-work, but the destructive Indian massacre of 1622 put an end to this enterprise.[1] In the beginning of the eighteenth century, under Governor Spotswood, the industry was resumed in this colony.[2] Maryland likewise produced pig and bar iron. About 1645 iron works were started in Lynn and Braintree in Massachusetts,[3] and proved very successful.[4] Iron was likewise produced in New York, but it was brittle.[5] This was the condition of affairs in the second decade of the eighteenth century. The Southern colonies were producing bar and pig iron, and exporting it to England in very small quantities.[6] The Northern colonies, and especially New England, produced iron in smaller quantities, but they were already, in connection with their ship-building and fisheries, beginning to make finished products out of the raw material.

But as yet the colonies were dependent on England for these commodities. On an average, between 1714 and 1717, the colonies imported from England £35,631 worth of wrought iron and nails.[7] They likewise imported unwrought iron from England, for the colonial mines could not supply the demand.[8] Thus New England imported from England

---

[1] Beverley's *Virginia*, i, p. 38, ii, p. 9; Swank, *History of Iron*, pp. 76–78.

[2] Letters of Spotswood, i, p. xiii; *cf.* Burnaby, p. 45; Anderson, iii, p. 285; Swank, *History of Iron*, pp. 198, 199.

[3] *Essex Institute*, xviii, p. 241.

[4] *Massachusetts Colonial Records*, ii, p. 103; *New York Colonial Documents*, iii, p. 113

[5] *New York Colonial Documents*, iv, p. 182.

[6] Scrivenor, p. 81.

[7] *New York Colonial Documents*, v, p. 617.   [8] *Ibid.*

in 1710, 200 tons of bar iron, and in 1715, 372 tons.[1]   The
other colonies also imported, but in smaller quantities.

The duties on iron in England were very heavy.   An export duty was charged on iron, both wrought and raw.[2]
Heavy import duties were laid on the metal when imported
into England, amounting by the various subsidies and the
impost of 1690,[3] to over two pounds a ton.[4]   To encourage
the iron manufacturers of England, iron wares reëxported
from England to the colonies were not allowed any drawback.[5]   And in 1721, for the further encouragement of the
British manufacturers, it was provided that all export duties on
iron should cease.[6]   Pig iron in the third decade began to be
sent from the colonies to England, and therefore, in the book
of rates of 1724, pig iron of the British plantations was rated
at only one pound per ton, paying thus a duty of about four
shillings per ton.[7]

In 1719 the first serious attempt to interfere with the iron
industry in the colonies was made.   In this year a bill was
introduced into the House of Commons providing, among
other things, that "none in the plantations should manufacture iron wares of any kind, out of any sows, pigs, or bars."[8]
The House of Lords added another clause, "that no forge
going by water, or other work whatsoever, should be erected
in any of the plantations, for making sows, pigs, or cast iron,
into bar or rod iron."[9]   To the relief of the colonies the bill
was dropped.

In 1728, Virginia and Maryland began exporting pig iron
in quantities to England.   During that year the two colonies

---

[1] Bishop, i, p. 629; French, *History of Iron*, p. 4.   [2]Saxby, p. 291.

[3] 2 Will. and Mary, *Stat.* 2, c. 4.   [4] Saxby, p. 107.

[5] 2 and 3 Anne, c. 9, § xii; 9 Anne, c. 6, § liv.

[6] 8 Geo. I., c. 15, § vii; Saxby, p. 291.   [7] 11 Geo. I., c. i; Saxby, p. 179.

[8] Macpherson, iii, p. 72; Scrivenor, p. 71.

[9] Macpherson, iii, pp. 72, 73; *Letter* (London, 1720), p. 12.

exported 852 tons, most of which was pig iron; in the same year Pennsylvania exported only 274 tons.[1] In 1730 Virginia and Maryland exported to England 2,081 tons, and Pennsylvania only 169 tons. In New England, on the other hand, what was produced was consumed there, and in addition quantities were imported. In 1729, New England imported 337 tons of bar iron; in 1731, 243 tons; and in 1734, 370 tons.[2] In New York about one-fourth of this quantity was imported, and into the other colonies scarcely any at all.[3]

As regards the iron industry, the distinction between the Northern and the Southern colonies is, that while the former manufactured more iron wares, the latter exported more raw iron and even partially supplied the Northern colonies with raw materials for the manufacture of iron wares.[4] Thus, in 1732, there were in New England six furnaces and nineteen forges for making iron.[5] Ordinary iron wares were produced in the colonies, but that imported from England was "wholely used by the shipping."[6] This statement is confirmed by a remark of Bennett's, made eight years later, in 1740. "There are," he says, "several iron mines, too, in New England, and some very large iron-works, which furnish them with iron for most of their ordinary uses; but the iron imported from England is counted the best, by far, to use about their shipping."[7]

[1] In 1730, 169 tons were exported from Pennsylvania to England.
In 1730, 2081 tons were exported from Virginia and Maryland to England.
In 1740, 159 tons were exported from Pennsylvania to England.
In 1740, 2025 tons were exported from Virginia and Maryland to England.
In 1745, 97 tons were exported from Pennsylvania to England.
In 1745, 2135 tons were exported from Virginia and Maryland to England.
French, *History of the Iron Trade*, pp. 7, 8; Bishop, i, p. 626.

[2] French, p. 5.   [3] *Ibid.*
[4] Swank, p. 91.   [5] Macpherson, iii, p. 189.
[6] Macpherson, iii, p. 188; *cf.* Anderson, iii, p. 291; *New York Colonial Documents*, v, p. 598.

[7] *Proceedings of the Massachusetts Historical Society*, 1860–1862, p. 111.

In 1750, the following general branches of the industry existed in New England: smelting furnaces, reducing the ore into pigs; refineries, that manufactured pig iron, made in the furnaces of New York, Pennsylvania and Maryland, into bars; slitting-mills for nails, plating-forges, and steel furnaces.[1] Such necessary commodities as scythes, anchors and fish-hooks, were made.[2] But New England always imported considerable quantities of wrought iron from England.[3] In New York, the iron industry was comparatively unimportant.[4] In New Jersey not much progress was made toward its establishment till about the middle of the eighteenth century. From and after 1740 numerous iron works were built in this commonwealth.[5] Pennsylvania exported, as mentioned above, much less raw iron than Virginia and Maryland. Unlike Massachusetts, scarcely any bar iron was imported, while wrought iron was imported in considerable quantities. Yet with the exception of Massachusetts, there were more forges in Pennsylvania than in any other commonwealth.[6]

As the colonies exported iron in increasing quantities to England, a controversy arose about the policy of allowing American iron to be brought into England free of duty. The quantity as yet imported from the colonies was insignificant when compared with the total amount imported;[7] but it was hoped that, freed from the onerous duty, the American iron industry would rapidly increase. Thus Gee writes, "they have several Times since applied for having the small Duty on Pig Iron taken off, but even that has not been done, and Bar Iron still continues to pay the Duty as

[1] Swank, pp. 91, 92; Bishop, i, p. 491.

[2] Weeden, p. 498.   [3] French, pp. 4–6.

[4] Swank, pp. 101–103.   [5] *Ibid.*, pp. 112, 113.

[6] French, pp. 4–6.   See also Swank; Ford, *Report of 1791*, p. 30.

[7] *Ibid.;* Dowell, iv, p. 460.

foreign Iron."[1] The English merchants maintained that inasmuch as England was forced to import iron, it would be much better to import it from the colonies and pay in manufactures, than to import it from Sweden and pay in metal.[2] The producers of bar iron in England said that if bar iron could be imported without paying duties, the English industry would be ruined by the competition, since fuel was so much cheaper in the colonies. The owners of wood lands maintained that their lands would decline in value,[3] and the tanners also feared that if fewer trees were felled, the price of bark would increase. Through this conflict of interest, nothing was done till 1750, and the bill which passed at that time was essentially a compromise.

The preamble is so typical of the spirit influencing English legislation that it deserves quotation in full. "Whereas," it reads, "the importation of bar iron from his Majesty's colonies in America, into the port of London, and the importation of pig iron from the said colonies, into any port of Great Britain, and the manufacture of such bar and pig iron in Great Britain, will be a great advantage not only to the said colonies, but also to this Kingdom, by furnishing the manufacturers of iron with a supply of that useful and necessary commodity, and by means thereof large sums of money, now annually paid for iron to foreigners, will be saved to this Kingdom, and a greater quantity of the Woollen, and other manufactures of Great Britain will be exported to America, in exchange for such iron imported," the following is enacted:[4]

I. Bar iron may be imported duty free to the port of London, and pig iron to any port of England.

---

[1] Gee, p. 69.   [2] French, p. 6.

[3] Gee, *The Trade and Navigation of Great Britain* (ed. 1731), p. 160.

[4] 23 Geo. II., c. 29.

II. No mill or other engine for rolling or slitting iron, no plating forge to work with a tilt-hammer, nor any furnace for making steel, shall be erected in the colonies. If so erected it is to be deemed a common nuisance. At first it had been intended to order the demolition of all existing forges in the colonies, but finally and by only a slender majority, the statute took this shape.[1]

Against the passage of this bill the tanners of Sheffield in Yorkshire protested, saying that " English iron would be undersold; consequently a great number of furnaces and forges would be discontinued; in that case the woods used for fuel would stand uncut, and the tanners be deprived of oak bark sufficient for the continuance and support of their occupation."[2] On the other hand, the ironmongers and smiths of Birmingham said that the bill would encourage their trade and would save money paid to Sweden. But they prayed at the same time that the erecting of forges and mills in the colonies might be restrained.[3]

The effects of the act were beneficial. In 1745, 2,228 tons of pig iron were exported from the colonies to England; in 1755, 3,425 tons.[4] In comparison with the total amount of imports of iron into England, this quantity was, however, very small.[5]

In 1756, the merchant adventurers of Bristol petitioned the House of Commons, that since great quantities of bar iron were imported from Sweden and Russia, and paid for in money, bar iron from the colonies might be imported into

---

[1] Bancroft (ed. 1878), iii, p. 42.

[2] Scrivenor, p. v.   [3] *Ibid.*, pp. 75, 76.

[4] French, p. 8; *cf. Dinwiddie Papers*, i, p. 386. Maryland exported iron through Virginia, since there was not enough shipping in this colony. *Correspondence of Gov. Sharpe*, ii, p. 15.

[5] Dowell, iv, p. 460.

any port of England free of duty.[1]   Many petitions supported
this request, and in many counter-petitions the danger of
such a policy was urged.[2]   In 1757, a statute provided that
bar iron might be imported free of duty into any port of
England.[3]   This act proved very beneficial.   While, in 1750,
the colonies exported scarcely any bar iron to England, and,
in 1754, only 271 tons; in 1764, they exported 1,059 tons.[4]

[1] Scrivenor, p. 76.   [2] *Ibid.*, pp. 76–80.
[3] 30 Geo. II., c. 16.   [4] Scrivenor, pp. 8, 10.

CHAPTER V. BOUNTIES AND OTHER ENCOURAGEMENTS OFFERED TO COLONIAL INDUSTRY AND COMMERCE BEFORE 1763.

§ 1. *Reasons for Encouraging the Production of Naval Stores.* We have seen above how unfavorable, in the eyes of the mercantilists, was the condition of the English iron trade with Sweden. When we consider the trade in naval stores we shall see that essentially the same dangerous conditions prevailed, only to an enhanced degree. From 1697 to 1701 the balance against England in her trade with Denmark, Norway, and Sweden, averaged annually £275,982.[1] Those countries supplied timber, tar, pitch, hemp and iron for England's ship-building industry. In 1716 Denmark, Norway, Sweden, and Russia exported to England 511,-000 pounds' worth of these commodities. In return England gave £262,000 in commodities, and the remainder in money. The balance against England was £249,000.[2] Nearly all the hemp used by England was furnished by Russia,[3] which country in one year exported hemp and flax to the value of £1,000,000.[4] Some time later, as Gee informs us, the balance against England in her trade with Norway was £130,-000, in her trade with Sweden £240,000, in her trade with Russia £400,000.[5]

To lessen this unfavorable trade, the mercantilists devised the plan of encouraging the production of naval stores in the

---

[1] Anderson, iii, p. 215.   [2] *Ibid*, iii, p. 294.

[3] Macpherson, iii, p. 74; Gee, p. 87; *Considerations on the Present State of our Northern Colonies* (London, 1763), p. 7.

[4] Anderson, iii, p. 223.   [5] Gee, pp. 121, 122.

colonies.[1] Thus in 1715 a New Englander wrote to the Board of Trade, "to prevent our setting up, in New England, manufactures that will interfere with Great Britain, it is highly necessary to employ the New England people as much as possible in making naval stores for their mother country, *lest they should hereafter be obliged to depend on the pleasure of the Danes, Swedes and Russians, for leave to set a fleet to sea.*"[2] As late as May 30th, 1765, Governor Bernard said: "Soon after my arrival to this government, I formed in my mind an idea of three improvements which this country was capable of making profitable to itself and convenient to Great Britain: I mean pot ash, hemp, and the carrying lumber to the British markets. They are all proper staples for New England, and must be very acceptable to Great Britain, *as she is at present supplied with them from foreigners by a losing trade.*"[3] These are examples of opinions expressed, and many more such might be furnished for earlier and intervening years.

In addition to this unfavorable trade with the Northern countries, there was likewise another reason why the production of naval stores in the colonies should be encouraged. Toward the end of the seventeenth century, England checked the nascent woolen industry in the colonies. The English statesmen and economists recognized, however, that the lack of a staple to export to England forced the colonists upon this course, for they had no commodity with which

[1] Already in 1664 it had been enacted that all hemp, tar and pitch imported from Virginia and Maryland into England should be freed from duties for five years. The purpose of this enactment was to divert the colonists from the precarious and immoral tobacco industry. Sainsbury, *Calendar*, 1661-1668, p. 257.

[2] Anderson, iii, p. 291; *cf.* also *Discourse of Trade* (London, 1697), p. 91; *Massachusetts Historical Society Collections*, 3d Series, vii, p. 242.

[3] *Speeches of the Governors of Massachusetts*, 1765-1775 (Boston, 1818), p. 33; *cf. An Enquiry into the Rights of the British Colonies*, by Richard Bland, of Virginia (London, 1769).

they could pay for the manufactures imported from England. Thus in the letters to the Board of Trade, we continually find advice to encourage some staple, for thereby the colonists will, of their own accord, cease from so unprofitable an industry as manufacturing. What commodities should be favored? Undoubtedly those which the colonies could easily produce, and which England had to purchase with great loss from the Northern nations; namely, naval stores.

A few quotations will show that this was the line of thought. Lord Cornbury, in a letter quoted above, says: "To Europe our people send Skins of all sorts, Whale Oyle and Bone," "but if they were encouraged, the people of this Province would be able to supply England with all manner of Naval Stores, Pitch, Tar, Rosine, Turpentine, Flax, Hemp, Mast and Timber." "If they had a sure market for Hemp and Flax in England, they would greedily fall to the planting of Hemp and Flax, *because they want commoditys, to make returns to England for the goods they take from thence.*"[1] In Anderson's work on commerce it is said: "Nothing will be able to prevent those people from manufactures interfering with ours, but their being constantly employed in raising naval stores, and other rough materials for our own manufactures, such as silk, flax, hemp, iron, &c."[2] The celebrated novelist, Daniel De Foe, embodies the same idea in one of his books. Encouraging naval stores, he writes, "would effectually furnish those Colonies with Returns for England, which they are now greatly distressed for, in order to pay the Ballance of their Trade with England."[3] In a letter published in 1720 we read, "but as the People of New England, New York, Pennsylvania, Carolina, &c.

[1] *Documentary History of New York,* i, p. 711.

[2] Anderson, iii, pp. 440, 441.

[3] De Foe, *A Plan of the English Commerce* (London, 1749), p. 359.

are under great Necessities for English Manufactures, and an Incapacity of providing Commodities to pay for them, has prevented the English Merchants from sending them those large Quantities that might be a Sufficient Supply; and as inevitable Necessity has put them upon manufacturing for themselves; therefore this New Employment of providing Naval Stores, was propos'd to take them off the Manufactures that interfere with ours."[1]

The unfavorable condition of British trade with the Baltic was one of the chief causes for the adoption of the policy of encouraging the production of naval stores in the colonies. Besides there was the recognition on the part of the English legislators that the colonies were being forced into manufacturing, owing to the fact that they had no staple wherewith to make returns to England. To give the Northern colonies such a staple, and thus keep them from manufacturing, it was decided to grant bounties on the importation of naval stores. In addition to these two fundamental reasons, there was the desire to promote the growth of the English navy.

The immediate occasion, however, of the first act encouraging the production of these commodities, was a change in the attitude of Sweden. At the beginning of the eighteenth century the Swedish Tar Company refused to let England have any pitch or tar except at its own price, even though money were offered in return. Swedish ships were to be used solely in transporting these commodities to England, and the company was to have the privilege of limiting the quantity so brought.[2] English statesmen recognized then how great a danger there was in depending on foreign countries for their military stores, for at this time England

---

[1] *A Letter to a Member of Parliament Concerning the Naval-Store Bill* (London, 1720), p. 14.

[2] Macpherson, ii, p. 724; *Letter, etc.* (London, 1720), pp. 4-7; Gee, pp. 83, 84.

was involved in a European war. Thus the English envoy to Sweden writes: "What Difficulties there are in making and bringing it (naval stores) from New England, I am not acquainted with, but take it for granted England had better give one third more for it from thence, than have it at such Uncertainties, and in so precarious a manner from other Countries, &c."[1] Therefore, at the beginning of the war of the Spanish Succession, a statute[2] was passed granting bounties on naval stores imported from the British colonies into England. These naval stores can be grouped under three categories, hemp, masts, tar and pitch; and for the sake of clearness, each category will be discussed in a separate section.

§ 2. *Hemp.* In this statute of Anne,[3] a bounty of £6 per ton was granted on hemp imported from the plantations into England. Since the statute was passed on account of the needs of the royal navy, as well as for other reasons, the commissioners were for twenty days to have the right of preëmption of all hemp so imported. By various statutes, this bounty was continued.[4] But hemp when imported into England still continued paying duties; in 1721, however, it was enacted that bright and clean hemp from the colonies, should be free of duty.[5] Later, the drawback on unwrought hemp exported from England to the colonies was taken away.[6] This provision was an indirect method of encouraging the production of hemp in the colonies, since it rendered the hemp imported from England the dearer.

Governors continually spoke of the especial fitness of the soil in the colonies for the production of hemp—yet all these

---

[1] *Letter* (London, 1720), p. 7.   [2] 3 and 4 Anne, c. 10.

[3] 3 and 4 Anne, c. 10, § ii.

[4] 12 Anne, *Stat.* i, c. 12; 8 Geo. I., c. 12, § i; 16 Geo. II., c. 26; 24 Geo. II., c. 57; 31 Geo. II., c. 35.

[5] 8 Geo. I., c. 12, § i.   [6] 4 Geo. II., c. 27, § vii.

attempts at raising hemp in any considerable quantity proved abortive.[1] In 1715 little hemp was made in New England,[2] while some was imported from England[3] and was used in New England's ship building industry. Efforts and plans for the encouragement of this industry continued throughout the colonial period.[4] They all proved of no avail. Thus Franklin writes, "did ever any North-American bring his hemp to England for this bounty? We have not yet enough for our own consumption. We begin to make our own cordage. You want to suppress that manufacture, and would do it by getting the raw material from us. You want to be supplied with hemp for your manufactures, and Russia demands money."[5]

§ 3. *Masts and the Protection of Woods, Duties on Lumber.* The same statute which granted a bounty on hemp provided that the importer of masts from the colonies should receive £1 for every ton.[6] To protect the woods in the colonies it was provided that a penalty of £15 should be imposed for the felling of pitch, pine, or tar trees under a certain size. And that the encouragement of the production of naval stores was meant to give the Northern colonies a commodity wherewith they could make returns to England, may per-

[1] Gee, pp. 145, 146; *Letter* (London, 1720), p. 32; Macpherson, iii, p. 215.

[2] Anderson, iii, p. 291.   [3] *New York Colonial Documents,* v, p. 616.

[4] *Considerations on the Present State of our Northern Colonies* (London, 1763), p. 12. This pamphlet was written solely to urge the colonists to raise hemp and flax. The ultimate end was to strengthen the navy against "those sulky Barbarians, who no doubt in a little time will feel their own Power, and from the same Inducement (tho' with greater Rapidity), like Goths and Vandals, overrun all Europe."

[5] Franklin, *Works,* iv, p. 225; *cf.* Sheffield, *Observations on the Commerce of the American States* (London, 1784), p. 48. Speaking of hemp, he says, "although an article of exportation from America, she does not raise a fiftieth part of her consumption."

[6] 3 and 4 Anne, c. 10; 12 Anne, *Stat.* i, c. 12; 2 Geo. II., c. 35, § iii.

haps be seen from the fact that this provision related only to the woods in New Hampshire,[1] Massachusetts Bay, Rhode Island, Providence Plantations, Connecticut, New York, and New Jersey.[2] This penalty proved inadequate. The surveyor-general of the woods marked certain trees with the broad arrow, signifying thereby that this tree was to be reserved for the use of the navy. Others, however, wishing to reserve certain trees for their private uses, marked them similarly. In 1709, Bridger, the surveyor-general, complained of the impossibility of getting a judgment against people for cutting trees.[3] Two years later, he wrote of the "great destruction of woods."[4]

The cutting of white or other pine trees, fit for masts, not being the property of private persons, except by royal license, was accordingly forbidden under a penalty of £100.[5] Likewise counterfeiting the broad arrow was punished by a fine of £5.[6] Later it was provided that no white pine trees outside the bounds of a township should be cut without a royal license. The penalties varied according to the size of the tree, from £5 to £50.[7] This statute was evaded by erecting large tracts of land into townships. To prevent this, a statute was passed providing that white pine trees might be felled only when on the property of private persons.[8]

As President Walker aptly says, "there was a long time in the life of the United States when 'the axe of the pioneer' was perhaps the best emblem of our civilization."[9] It was claimed that these restrictions hindered the clearing of land, the first step in the civilization of a virgin country. Thus in

---

[1] It should, however, be remembered that at this time it was thought that the best pine trees were in the North; compare Gee, p. 54.

[2] 3 and 4 Anne, c. 10, § iv.   [3] Chalmers, *Revolt*, i, p. 323.   [4] *Ibid.*, p. 324.

[5] 9 Anne, c. 17, § i.   [6] *Ibid.*, § ii.   [7] 8 Geo. I., c. 12, § v.

[8] 2 Geo. II., c. 35, § i.   [9] *Yale Review*, i, p. 125.

New York the planter was at one time placed in an awkward dilemma. For land in this colony was granted on condition that three out of every fifty acres be cleared within three years.[1]

Lumber imported into England from the colonies paid the same duties as lumber from foreign countries; and as England imported much lumber, it was proposed to take this duty off the colonial product. The scarcity of wood in England began in the days of the Tudors.[2] William Harrison, writing in the reign of Elizabeth, says, "it should seem by ancient records, and the testimony of sundry authors, that the whole countries of Lhoegres and Cambria, now England and Wales, have sometimes been very well replenished with great woods and groves, although at this time the said commodity be not a little decayed in both, and in such wise that a man shall oft ride ten or twenty miles in each of them and find very little, or rather none at all, except it be near unto towns, gentlemen's houses, and villages."[3]

For her various industries, England imported considerable quantities of lumber from the other European countries. A great amount was used as fuel for the iron industry; the construction of ships likewise required much wood. From Sweden, Denmark, Norway, Holland, and Germany, England imported masts, planks, staves and boards.[4] In view of the prevailing economic doctrines, it would be far more to England's commercial advantage to buy these commodities from the colonies, in return for woolens and other manufactures.

---

[1] *Documentary History of New York*, i, p. 719. This complaint was made by Cadwallader Colden in 1723.

[2] *Cf. Britannia Languens* (London, 1680), p. 52.

[3] *Elizabethan England;* from "A Description of England," by William Harrison (in "Holinshed's Chronicles"), ed. Withington, p. 196.

[4] Gee, pp. 16, 17, 54.

In 1700 Penn proposed that imposts be laid on foreign timber, so as to encourage the importation of this product from the colonies.[1] The merchants trading with the colonies urged the adoption of this policy, saying that when the tobacco or rice crops fell short, many ships had either to return to England dead-freighted, or else to wait there for the next crop. If the importation of colonial timber were encouraged, they would always be sure of a cargo.[2] Therefore in the third decade of the eighteenth century it was provided that all kinds of timber could be imported into England from the colonies free of duty.[3]

Of the effects of this statute, Gee writes nine years later, " when our Ships go to Virginia or the other Colonies, if they cannot meet with a full Loading, they now fill up their Ships with Pipe-staves, Boards, and Timber of several Kinds ; by which Means they often make quicker Voyages ; whereas before they sometimes lay in the Country Six, Eight, or Ten Months, whilst the Worms were eating out their Bottoms."[4]

The finest masts were obtained in New England ; Massachusetts at one time presented some of exceptional size to Charles II.[5] " The British Navy for Eighty years before the late war," says Belknap, " received its masts wholly from America."[6] Yet the value and importance of this trade was only a relative one ; for the masts sent to England from the colonies in 1769 were worth at the place of exportation only £7819.[7] Nor was the quantity of lumber sent to England very considerable. The amount of lumber sent to Spain, Portugal and the West Indies was much greater.[8]

[1] *New York Colonial Documents*, iv, p. 757.

[2] Macpherson, iii, p. 72; Gee, p. 91.

[3] 8 Geo. I., c. 12, § ii.   This statute was continued by others.

[4] Gee, p. 14.   [5] *New York Colonial Documents*, iii, pp. 140, 141, 182.

[6] Belknap's *New Hampshire*, p. 155.   [7] Sheffield, p. 83.   [8] *Ibid.*, p. 68.

§ 4. *Tar, Pitch, Turpentine and Rosin*.   Under Anne the following bounties were offered for the importation of these commodities into England:

I. Tar, per ton four pounds.

II. Pitch, per ton four pounds.

III. Rosin and turpentine, per ton three pounds.[1]

Later it was enacted that the queen could appropriate £10,000 for the employment of skillful persons, and for furnishing utensils and materials for carrying out the design of raising naval stores.[2]   The commissioner of the royal navy had for twenty days the right of preëmption of these commodities so imported.   To ensure tar and pitch of bad quality from getting the bounty, the officers of the customs were to examine them to see if they were good and merchantable and not mixed with dirt.[3]   Later it was provided that no premiums should be granted for tar, unless there was a certificate from the governor that the tar had been made in a prescribed manner.[4]   The cause of this was that the tar of the plantations was too hot and burned the cordage.   This complaint was a universal one.

Early in George II.'s reign, after the expiration of the former statute, the bounties were lessened:

I. Pitch, per ton one pound.

II. Turpentine, per ton one pound eight shillings.

III. Tar, per ton two pounds four shillings.[5]

IV. But if tar was made in the prescribed manner it was to receive the same bounty as before.[6]

The method prescribed was borrowed from that in use in Russia[7] and Sweden,[8] and this method[9] was ordered to be

---

[1] 3 and 4 Anne, c. 10, § ii.   [2] 8 Anne, c. 13, § xxx.   [3] 5 Geo. I., c. ii, § xvii.

[4] 8 Geo. I., c. 12, § iv.   [5] 2 Geo. II., c. 35, §iii.   [6] *Ibid.*, c. 35, § xi.

[7] *Documentary History of New York*, i, p. 723; *New York Colonial Documents*, v, p. 533.   [8] *New York Colonial Documents*, v, p. 479.

[9] 8 Geo. I., c. 12, § iv.   "When such trees were fit to bark, the bark thereof

employed because the colonial tar was so hot.[1] This method, however, did not meet with much success.[2] The tar produced in the colonies, except in this particular that it burned the cordage, was as good as that produced in the states of Northern Europe.[3] Thus Lord Sheffield in 1784 wrote, "the question as to the superor quality of the Baltic tar over the American, seems not perfectly decided." And he adds that although the former was preferred by some cordage makers, yet the latter was more adapted to other industries, and for those purposes commanded a higher price.[4]

In contrast to the meagre results obtained from the bounties on hemp and masts, those on pitch and tar were very successful.[5] These commodities soon began to be produced in all the colonies from New England to Georgia.[6] The amount imported by England from the colonies increased rapidly. In 1717 the tar, pitch, and turpentine sent annually to England was worth £47,072.[7] England soon had not only enough for her own consumption, but even exported these commodities to other countries.[8] Thus in 1719 an anonymous author writes, "we receive twice as

---

was stript eight foot, or thereabouts, up from the root of each tree, a slip of the bark of about four inches in breadth having been left on one side of each tree; and that each tree, after having been so bark'd, had stood during one year at the least, and was not before cut down for the making of tar; anything herein, or in any former law, to the contrary notwithstanding."

[1] Hawks, *History of North Carolina*, ii, p. 237; *New York Colonial Documents*, v, p. 118; Saunders, *Colonial Records of North Carolina*, iv, pp. 5, 6; p. 16.

[2] *New York Colonial Documents*, v, p. 479; *Documentary History of New York*, i, p. 723.

[3] *New York Colonial Documents*, v, p. 118.

[4] Sheffield, pp. 73, 74; *cf.* M'Culloch, *Dictionary of Commerce*, p. 1358.

[5] Anderson, iii, p. 291.			[6] Force, *Tracts*, ii, No. xii, p. x.

[7] *New York Colonial Documents*, v, p. 616.

[8] Gee, pp. 90, 145; Anderson, iii, p. 319; Sheffield, p. 70.

much as the Nation consumes, and are thereby enabled to export great quantities to the Streights, Spain, Portugal, Holland, Bremen, and Hamburg."[1]

The increased production of the commodities soon caused a rapid decline in their price.[2] By 1719 the price had already declined to one-third of what it had been twenty years before.[3]

In one respect the bounties were not successful, for they did not give the Northern colonies a staple to send to England. The great pine forests were in the South, and especially in the Carolinas. Although the other colonies[4] sent these commodities to England, the greater part came from the two Carolinas.[5] Thus Governor Johnson writes in 1734 to the Board of Trade, " there is more pitch and tar made in the two Carolinas than in all the other Provinces on the Continent and rather more in this than in South Carolina."[6] North Carolina soon began to push rapidly ahead of her sister colony in this industry. In 1770 the colonies exported to England 87,561 barrels of tar, 15,793 barrels of pitch, 41,-709 barrels of turpentine.[7] The greatest part came, however, from North Carolina.[8]

It is difficult to estimate how much of this development was due to the English bounties. The natural conditions for the prosperity of this industry were present, and the bounties undoubtedly aided its growth, especially at the commencement. Thus we are told that when the bounty on pitch and

---

[1] *Letter* (London, 1720), pp. 8, 9.   *Vide* Mitchell, *The Present State of Great Britain and North America*, London, 1767, p. 129.

[2] Ashley, *Considerations*, part i, p. 25; Franklin, Works, iv, p. 226.

[3] *Letter* (London, 1720), p. 9.   [4] *Dinwiddie Papers*, i, p. 386.

[5] Chalmers, *Revolt*, p. 323 n.; Force, *Tracts*, ii, "A Description of South Carolina," p. 6; Anderson, iii, p. 463; Macpherson, iii, p. 302.

[6] Saunders, *Colonial Records of North Carolina*, iv, p. 5.

[7] Sheffield, p. 69.   [8] *Ibid.*; Lindsay, *History of Merchant Shipping*, ii, p. 238.

tar was not paid for a few years, the Swedes gained again, and the policy of granting bounties had to be continued.[1]

§ 5. *Bounties on Indigo.* During the first half of the seventeenth century, England imported considerable quantities of indigo from the French West Indies.[2] Early in the history of South Carolina, attempts had been made to raise this commodity, but they had soon been abandoned.[3] About 1740 the production of indigo was reintroduced into South Carolina by Miss Lucas.[4] The industry grew very rapidly and soon indigo formed an essential factor in the exports of the Carolinas and of Georgia. The merchants trading to Carolina thereupon petioned parliament for a bounty on indigo imported into England from the colonies.[5] From November, 1747, to November, 1748, 134,118 lbs. of indigo[6] were exported from Charleston, and since indigo was an enumerated commodity, nearly all was sent to England. In view of the future possibility that this industry might free England from her dependence on the French for this commodity, parliament passed an act in 1748. This act granted a bounty of six pence a pound on indigo

---

[1] Postlethwayt's *Savary's Dictionary*, i, p. 534. Gee, pp. 144, 145, of *The Trade and Navigation of Great Britain Considered*, "......our Attempt upon Pitch and Tar; for the Encouragement whereof, a large Bounty was given for several Years, till it came to be imported in such vast Quantities, that we had not only enough for our own Consumption, but even to export to our Neighbours; from which great Plenty, we were ready to persuade ourselves, that this Business was sufficiently established, and therefore neglected the Continuance of the Bounty. Since which the Importation of those Commodities from Russia, Sweden, and Norway is re-assumed, etc."

[2] Ramsay, *South Carolina*, ii, p. 211; Ashley, part ii, p. 73; Macpherson, iii, p. 260.

[3] *Historical Collections of North Carolina*, ii, p. 69; Gee, p. 21.

[4] Ramsay, ii, p. 209; see Raynal, *Histoire des Indes*, iii, p. 351; vii, p. 404.

[5] Ramsay, ii, p. 211; Macpherson, iii, p. 260.

[6] *Historical Collections of South Carolina*, ii, p. 235; *cf.* Macpherson, iii, p. 260; Bishop, i, p. 348.

imported into England directly from any of the British colonies in America.[1]

The policy adopted was very successful, for the colonies soon supplied England and even competed with the French in some of the European markets.[2] The amount exported to England increased very rapidly.[3] In 1/69 the colonies exported to England 423,563 lbs;[4] in 1772 the Carolinas exported to the same country 1,107,600 lbs, while Georgia exported only 55,380 lbs.[5]

In addition to these bounties on hemp, masts, tar, and indigo, there were bounties offered for the production of other commodities. Then Virginia in 1669 offered fifty pounds of tobacco for every pound of wound silk made in the colony.[6] The societies for the improvement of arts and manufactures in England also offered bounties for the production of certain articles in the plantations.[7] But these bounties, forming no integral part of England's colonial policy, and being as a rule very unsuccessful, are foreign to our subject. Likewise there were bounties for the whale fisheries, but as these bounties were aimed especially to encourage the English industry, and only secondarily those of the colonies, they need not be discussed here.

§ 6. *Duties and Drawbacks.* As regards customs duties and drawbacks, the colonies were placed on the same footing as foreign states, that is, the general rules and regulations in regard to these matters applied both to foreign and colonial products.

As a rule, colonial products imported into England paid the same customs duties as the corresponding foreign pro-

[1] 21 Geo. II., c. 30, § i; 28 Geo. II., c. 25, § i.   [2] Ramsay, ii, p. 212.

[3] Ramsay, ii, p. 212; Bishop, i, pp. 348, 349.   [4] Sheffield, p. 96.

[5] Sheffield, Table No. i; Ramsay, ii, p. 212, Bishop, i, p. 349.

[6] Hening, ii, p. 272.

[7] Albert S. Bolles, *Industrial History of the United States*, p. 8; see Bishop, i.

ducts. To this rule there were, however, many exceptions. As mentioned above, colonial tobacco paid, on importation into England, a much lower rate of duty than Spanish tobacco.[1] Later pig and bar iron from the colonies were admitted into England free of all duties.[2] Hemp and lumber imported from the colonies, likewise paid no duties.[3] Molasses from the English colonies was exempted from the impost of 1690.[4] Whale-fins and train oil, if imported in colonial vessels, paid lower rates of duty than if imported in foreign shipping.[5] Indigo from the British plantations paid less than foreign indigo, until in George I.'s reign, both kinds were freed from all customs duties.[6] To encourage the production of silk in the colonies, raw-silk was allowed to be imported thence free of duty.[7] The next year, 1751, a statute permitted the importation of pearl and pot ashes from the colonies under the same condition.[8]

Commodities exported to the colonies were charged, as a rule, with the same export duties as commodities exported to foreign states. To this rule, again, there were exceptions. The duties on coals exported to the colonies were considerably lower than those on coals exported to foreign countries.[9] Tea could also be exported to the colonies without paying inland duties.[10] Then coffee produced in the British plantations paid a lower inland duty than coffee of foreign countries.[11]

The English system of drawbacks was a very complicated one. One-half of the duties payable by the "old subsidy" of 1660 was repaid on reëxportation of the commodity, while on the other hand the whole duty granted by the

[1] *Vide* above, pp. 27, 49.   [2] *Vide* above, p. 88.   [3] *Vide* above, p. 99.

[4] Saxby, pp. 32, 195.   [5] Saxby, pp. 40, 200, 201.   [6] Saxby, pp. 37, 177.

[7] 23 Geo. II., c. 20.   [8] 24 Geo. II., c. 51.

[9] 15 Charles II., c. 7, §§ x, xi; 9 Anne, c. 6, §§ v, vii; 12 Anne, *Stat.* 2, c. 9, §§ ix, xi; *cf.* Saxby, pp. 283, 284.

[10] 21 Geo. II., c. 14.   [11] 5 Geo. II., c. 24, § i; 25 Geo. II., c. 35, § i.

numerous other subsidies and imposts was repaid, if the commodity were reëxported. And, as the duty granted by the subsidy of 1660 was small in comparison with the sum total of all the other duties, the drawback practically amounted to nearly the whole duty. All but two and a half per cent. of the commodity, as in the book of rates, was paid back.

While this was the general rule, exceptions were made in favor of certain industries. Thus the whole duty on colonial tobacco was repaid.[1] To make the planters grow their own hemp, no drawback was allowed on unwrought hemp, reexported to the colonies from England.[2] Beaver skins were not allowed as large a drawback as other commodities.[3] Iron and iron wares exported to the British plantations were also to have no drawback.[4] This provision was meant to encourage the English manufacturer and the colonial producer.

The inhabitants of England complained of this system of drawbacks, saying that the colonist was thereby able to get certain foreign commodities more cheaply than they could be purchased in England. Thus linens were imported in great quantities into England from Holland and Germany. On account of the heavy duties paid in England, these commodities could not compete with the Irish and English goods. Nearly all was reëxported to the British colonies.[5] This great consumption of foreign linens in the colonies, rendered possible only by the drawback, naturally diminished the consumption of English linens, and according to Adam Smith, materially hurt the English linen industry.[6]

---

[1] *Cf.* above, p. 48.   [2] *Cf.* above.   [3] 8 Geo. I., c. 15, § xiv.

[4] *Cf.* above; Saxby, p. 179.   [5] Anderson, iii, p. 445; Roscher, p. 254.

[6] Adam Smith, *The Wealth of Nations*, ii, p. 165.

CHAPTER VI.   THE MOLASSES ACT.

§ 1. *Origin and Importance of the West India Trade.*   Although as far back as the reign of Edward IV.[1] we can find traces of the policy of restricting the importation of foreign grain into England, this policy was not definitely adopted until the reign of Charles II.   During this reign various statutes were passed, practically prohibiting the importation of foreign corn and wheat,[2] and by them, as well as by other laws of a similar nature, the Northern colonies were prevented from sending their normal products to England.   After the passage of these laws two courses were open to the Northern colonies.   They could manufacture for themselves and thus partially cease to purchase English manufactures.   When, however, the colonists threatened to pursue this course, various statutes put an end to the most serious attempts in this direction.   The other course, which was the more natural one, had thus of necessity to be fully adopted.   This was to export provisions to a third market, and with the money and commodities obtained thence to buy manufactures in England.   This intermediate market would be found most naturally in the West Indies, with which the colonies had already in 1660 commercial intercourse.   These islands, especially after this date, when their important development began, needed vast quantities of provisions, and produced commodities most acceptable in England.   In 1731 it was said, " by this trade the Northern colonies are enabled to make such considerable remittances to England in ready money, as

[1] Faber, *Die Entstehung des Agrarschutzes in England,* p. 85.
[2] Faber, pp. 103, 107; Thornton, *Historical Summary of the Corn Laws,* pp. 1–9.

they could procure nowhere else but by their traffic with the foreign colonies, as well as by indigo, cacao, sugar, and rum, both from British and foreign colonies, [in the West Indies], for enabling them to pay for the great quantities of our manufactures which they yearly take of us."[1]

The most important trade carried on by the Northern colonies was that with the West Indies; it was essential to their very existence. Thus the novelist De Foe writes, "without this export, those Colonies would perish."[2] In addition, Gee writes, "as the *Substance of the Colonies is the supplying our sugar Plantatians* with Flower, Bisket, Pipe-staves, Fish, and other Provisions, *prohibiting them that Commerce would be their utter Ruin.*"[3] A law to check this trade would be in direct opposition to the laws prohibiting manufactures, for if the colonies could not export their staple products to an intermediate market, they could not purchase manufactures from England. By this trade alone could the Northern colonists obtain sufficient money and commodities to pay for the importations from England. The amount of lumber, fish, and grain consumed by Spain and Portugal, and by the tobacco and rice colonies[4] was utterly inadequate for this purpose. Thus in 1764 Colden wrote, "it is evident to a demonstration that the more Trade the Colonies in North America have with the Foreign Colonies, the more they consume of the British Manufactures."[5]

A passage from a letter of Robert R. Livingston to Benjamin Franklin, written in 1782, shows very clearly the relation between this trade and the policy of prohibiting manufactures in

---

[1] Macpherson, iii, p. 175.

[2] *A Plan of English Commerce* (London, 1741), p. 356.

[3] Gee (ed. 1731), p. 72.

[4] *Cf. Works of D'Avenant*, ii, p. 21; Wood, *A Survey of Trade*, p. 145; *Documentary History of New York*, i, p. 716.

[5] *New York Colonial Documents*, vii, p. 612.

the colonies. "Without a free admission of all kinds of provisions into the Islands," he writes, " our agriculture will suffer extremely." . . . " It will lessen the consumption of foreign sugars, increase the supplies which the poorer people among us draw from the maple, &c., and by reducing the price of provision, and rendering the cultivation of lands less profitable, make proportionable increase of our own manufactures, and lessen our dependance on Europe."[1] From what has been said above, the justice of Mr. Edwards' contention will appear self-evident. In his history of the West Indies, he writes, " it may, I think, be affirmed, without hazard of contradiction, that if ever there was any one particular branch of commerce in the world, that called less for restraint and limitation than any other, it was the trade which previous to the year 1774 was carried on between the planters of the West Indies and the inhabitants of North America."[2]

§ 2. *Trade of the Northern Colonies with the West Indies.* The West India islands, belonging to England, France, Spain, Denmark and Holland, saw that their economic advantage consisted in the production of those commodities which were especially adapted to their soil and climate. These commodities were mainly sugar, molasses, rum and indigo. The whole energy of the islanders was devoted to the raising of these products, for they found that they could obtain their provisions and other necessaries of life with less

---

[1] Sparks, *Diplomatic Correspondence of the Revolution*, iv, p. 13; *cf.* also *Remonstrance of Rhode Island*, 1764: "As there is no commodity raised in the colony suitable for the European market, but the few articles aforementioned; and as the other goods raised for exportation, will answer at no market but in the West Indies, it necessarily follows that the trade thither must be the foundation of all our commerce; and it is undoubtedly true that solely from the prosecution of this trade with the other branches that are pursued in consequence of it, arises the ability to pay for such quantities of British goods." *Rhode Island Colonial Records*, vi, p. 379.

[2] *History of the West Indies* (London, 1793), ii, p. 393.

economic effort if they imported them, than if they themselves produced them.   The English colonies to the North of Maryland performed the function of supplying them with these necessary commodities.   In return for sugar they gave the West Indies fish and flour.   The exports of the Southern colonies, Virginia, Maryland and the Carolinas, to the islands were insignificant in comparison with those from New York, Pennsylvania, and New England.[1]   As the economic conditions of New England and the Middle colonies differentiated, so their exports to the West Indies came gradually to differ in character.   The chief export of New England became fish, while the Middle colonies sent mainly flour and bread.   Both sections sent cattle, horses, and especially lumber.

In the seventeenth century New England had produced considerable quantities of grain, especially wheat.   This she exported to the West Indies in return for the products of those islands.[2]   As, however, the fisheries became important, agriculture declined in the Northernmost colonies.   Soon New England ceased to produce a large surplus product of wheat, and was even at times forced to import it from the Middle colonies.[3]   Hence fish came gradually to be the chief article exported thence to the islands.   Thus in 1687 a French Protestant refugee writes of Boston, " this Town carries on a great Trade with the Islands of America and with Spain.   They carry to the Islands Flour, Salt Beef, Salt Pork, Cod, Staves, Salt Salmon, Salt Mackarel, Onions,

[1] *Cf.* Chalmers, *Revolt*, ii, p. 70; *Historical Collections of South Carolina*, ii, p. 226; *Spotswood Letters*, i, pp. 18, 87.

[2] *Hutchinson Papers* (Prince Society), ii, p. 150; ii, p. 230; Child, *A New Discourse of Trade* (London, 1694), p. 213; *cf.* Sainsbury's *Calendar*, 1661–1668, p. 167.

[3] *Massachusetts Historical Society Collection*, 4th Series, vii, p. 318; *New York Colonial Documents*, v, p. 686.

and Oysters salted in Barrels, great quantities of which are taken here."[1]   A few years later, in 1700, Higginson wrote, "we trade to all parts where the law doth not prohibit.   Our principal commodities are dry merchandise, cod-fish fit for the markets of Spaine, Portugal, the Straits, also refuse dry fish, mackerel, lumber, horses and provisions for the West Indies."[2]

The West India trade gradually became essential to the prosperity of the New England fisheries.   On the same voyage two qualities of fish were caught.   The better kind was sent to Spain and Portugal, and in smaller quantities to the English West Indies.[3]   From Spain and Portugal New England obtained salt for curing the fish, but mainly money, with which to pay England for the manufactures imported thence.[4]   The poorer quality of fish found a ready market in the foreign West India islands, where it was exchanged for rum, molasses, and sugar.[5]   As both kinds of fish were obtained on the same voyage, the prosperity of the New England fisheries demanded a market for the poorer kind of fish, as well as one for the superior quality.

Besides fish, New England exported great quantities of lumber to the islands.   Pipe-staves, masts,[6] and even ships[7]

[1] Fisher, *Report of a French Protestant Refugee in Boston*, 1687 (Brooklyn 1868), p. 23.

[2] *Massachusetts Historical Society Collections*, 3rd series, vii, p. 218.

[3] Bernard, *Select Letters*, p. 3; Sainsbury, *Calendar*, 1661-1668, p. 532.

[4] *New York Colonial Documents*, v, p. 595.

[5] *Speeches of the Governors of Massachusetts*, pp. 9–11; Macpherson, iii, p. 165. In 1778, John Adams wrote, "One part of our fish went to the West India Islands for rum, and molasses to be distilled into rum, which injured our health and our morals; the other part went to Spain and Portugal for gold and silver, almost the whole of which went to London, sometimes for valuable articles of clothing, but too often for lace and ribands."   Sparks' *Diplomatic Correspondence of the Revolution*, iv, p. 273.

[6] *Hutchinson Papers*, ii, p.150; *Massachusetts Historical Society Collections*, 2nd Series, ii, p. 218; Edwards, *West Indies*, ii, pp. 394, 395; Bernard, *Select Letters*, p. 10; Macpherson, iii, p. 166.

[7] Macpherson, iii, p. 189.

were sent there for sale.   Horses, oxen, pork and beef were likewise exported thither.[1]

As fish was the chief article of export from New England to the West Indies, agricultural products were the chief commodities exported from the Middle colonies.   These products were flour, bread, peas, bacon, and butter.[2]   In addition, pork, horses, cattle and especially lumber were exported.[3]

It was on account of this trade that we find in contemporary English writers so much dislike of the Northern colonies. Josiah Child lays down the proposition that " New England is the most prejudicial Plantation to this Kingdom."[4]   His reason is that, while the other plantations produce commodities of a different nature from those of England, such as tobacco or sugar, New England produces the same commodities as old England, corn and cattle.[5]   With these commodities she supplied Jamaica and Barbadoes " to the diminution of the vent of those Commodities from this Kingdom and to the lowering of the value of English lands."[6]

In this trade the balance was favorable to the Northern colonies, and money continually flowed into them from the West Indies.[7]   This was especially true of the trade with the

---

[1] *Massachusetts Historical Society Collections*, 2nd series, ii, pp. 218, 219; *Massachusetts Historical Society Proceedings*, 1860–1862, p. 111; Long, *Jamaica*, i, p. 501; Andros Tracts, ii, p. 114.

[2] *Documentary History of New York*, i, p. 711; i, p. 714, 715.   *New York Colonial Documents*, v, p. 601; v. p. 604; Gee, p. 23.

[3] *New York Colonial Documents*, v, p. 601; v, p. 51; v, p. 556.   *Documentary History of New York*, iv, pp. 182, 183; Campbell, *Sugar Trade*, p. 220; Macpherson, iii, p. 147.

[4] *A New Discourse on Trade*, p. 212.   [5] *Ibid.*, p. 213.

[6] *Ibid.*, p. 214; *cf.* also Whitworth, *Scarce Tracts* (London, 1778), [Carew Reynell, *True English Interest*, 1674], p. 192; Cary, *A Discourse on Trade*, (London, 1745), p. 51; *Hutchinson Papers*, ii, p. 231.

[7] Fisher, *Report of French Protestant Refugee*, p. 23; *Documentary History of New York*, i, p. 714; *New York Colonial Documents*, v, p. 58.

Dutch colony Curaçoa,[1] and with Jamaica.[2]   With the money thus obtained, either in the form of bills of exchange or metal, the colonies paid England for her manufactures.   But as the balance of trade with the mother country was continually against the colonies, the money obtained in the West India trade had soon to be sent away to pay for English goods.[3]   Thus towards the end of the colonial period Colden writes, " but whatever advantages we have by the West India trade we are so hard put to it to make even with England, that the money imported from the West Indies seldom continues six months in the province, before it is remitted for England.[4]"

Some of the commodities purchased in the islands by the Northern colonies were also sent to England to pay for the manufactures consumed in those colonies.[5]   Thus Child says of these colonies, " the other Commodities we have from them, as some few great Masts, Furs and Train-Oyle, whereof the Yearly value amounts to very little, the much greater value of returns from thence, being made in Sugar, Cotton, Wool, Tobacco, and such like Commodities, which they first receive from some other of his Majesties Plantations, in Barter for dry Cod-fish, salt Mackarel, Beef, Pork, Bread, Beer, Flower, Pease."[6]   A few years later Higginson wrote of Massachusetts, "the returns made directly hence for England, are chiefly sugar, molasses, cotton, wool, logwood and brazilla-wood; for which we are beholden to the West Indies."[7]   Many New England ships sailed directly from the islands to England.[8]

---

[1] *Massachusetts Historical Society Collections*, 2nd series, ii, p. 219.   *The Importance of the British Plantations*, p. 94.

[2] Long, *Jamaica*, i, pp. 504, 539.   [3] Campbell, *Sugar Trade*, p. 222.

[4] *New York Colonial Documents*, v, p. 686.   [5] *Ibid.*, v, p. 51.

[6] *A New Discourse of Trade*, p. 213.

[7] *Massachusetts Historical Society Collections*, 3rd series, vii, p. 218.

[8] Macpherson, iii, p. 166.

When, in 1766, at the time of the Stamp Act troubles Benjamin Franklin was examined before a committee of the House of Commons, he was asked some questions about the trade of Pennsylvania.   He said Pennsylvania imported from England commodities to the value of £500,000, while she produced only £40,000 worth of commodities for direct exportation to England.   In answer to the surprise expressed at such a remarkable disproportion, he said that Pennsylvania made up the balance by her trade with the English, French, Spanish, Dutch and Danish West Indies.[1]

Later the trade routes became even more complex and roundabout.   The molasses imported from the islands was made into rum in New England.   In 1731 it was stated that in one year New England made 1,260,000 gallons of rum.[2] This was used both in the Indian trade and in the fishing industry.[3]   It was also sent in great quantities to the African coast and there exchanged for slaves.[4]   The slaves were sold in the Southern plantations, or in the West Indies, and the money obtained from the traffic went to England to pay for manufactures.   Thus in 1764, it was said that for the last thirty years eighteen vessels had annually sailed from the colony of Rhode Island for the Gold Coast.   These vessels were laden with rum, and in exchange for it slaves were purchased.   The merchants then sold the slaves in Carolina, Virginia and the West Indies, receiving bills of exchange in return.   By this trade alone Rhode Island was able to pay debts in England to the amount of £40,000 a year.[5]

[1] *Parliamentary History* (ed. London, 1813), xvi, p. 139; *cf.* also J. Dickinson's *Political Writings* (Wilmington, 1801), p. 51.

[2] Macpherson, iii, p. 176; Anderson, iii, p. 438.   [3] *Ibid.*

[4] Raynal, vii, p. 9; Smith, *Wealth of Nations*, ii, p. 159; Chamberlain, *Winsor*, vi, p. 9.

[5] *Rhode Island Colonial Records*, vi, p. 380.

§ 3. *Jealousy of the French West Indies—The Molasses Act.* Already in 1661 the inhabitants of Barbadoes petitioned against the enumeration of sugar.[1] It was claimed that the enumeration was detrimental, especially as the land had become poorer.[2] In 1664 the same island again complained of the Act of Navigation, saying that while the English were declining, the French were becoming more and more prosperous.[3] In the same year, though a little later, Antigua urged that the English were still declining while the French had grown to "numerousness and riches."[4] A few years later these complaints were repeated.[5]

The rapid development of the French West Indies was checked by the new colonial policy adopted in France. In 1668 the Company of the West Indies was granted a monopoly of trade to the islands.[6] Subsequently more restrictive measures were introduced. The most grievous was the provision that raw sugar from the colonies should not be reëxported from France.[7] This measure found its support in the purely mercantile argument, that France should not furnish her commercial rivals with raw materials, for thereby in the end she would harm herself.[8] Heavy duties rendered the production of sugar burdensome.[9] This policy resulted in a decline of the prosperity of the French islands, which con-

---

[1] Sainsbury, Calendar, 1661–1668, pp. 29, 30.

[2] *Ibid.*, p. 45.   [3] *Ibid.*, pp. 229, 230.

[4] *Ibid.*, p. 234.   [5] *Ibid.*, p. 542.

[6] *Arrêt du conseil portant que le commerce des îles ne sera fait que par la compagnie des Indes occidentales, ou par les bâtimens françois, avec la permission de cette compagnie. Recueil Général des anciennes Lois Françaises*, xviii, p. 196.

[7] Leroy–Beaulieu, p. 166.

[8] Raynal, vii, p. 17.

[9] *Memorials presented by the Deputies of the Council of Trade in France to the Royal Council in 1701* (London, 1737), p. 13; Postlethwayt's *Savary, Universal Dictionary of Trade and Commerce* (London, 1757), i, p. 853.

tinued from the first peace of Aix-la-Chapelle to the peace of Rastadt.[1]

It was not until after the war of the Spanish secession that a complete change was brought about in French colonial policy, due, according to Leroy-Beaulieu, to the financier John Law.[2] This policy inaugurated in 1717 was a comparatively liberal one.[3] Besides other alleviations, it was provided that all provisions and forms of merchandise, designed for exportation to the French island colonies, should be exempted from duties.[4] Then, with certain limitations, all goods from the French colonies might be reëxported from France subject to a duty of three per cent.[5] This liberal policy enabled the French West Indies to make most rapid progress in the development of the sugar industry.

About this time also the Northern colonies in America had so increased in size that the English West Indies were no longer able to take all their surplus commodities. Hence a most profitable trade sprang up between the French islands and the English colonies, and as the prosperity of the latter increased, their trade with the foreign islands became even more necessary. As the continental colonies were capable of indefinite territorial expansion, while the development of the small island colonies was, by the very nature of things, restricted, the British West Indies could by no means

---

[1] *Ce ne fut qu'au xviii* *siècle que les îles françaises furent placées dans les conditions les plus favorables pour la production du sucre ; jusque là et spécialement sous Colbert des réglements oppressifs arrêtèrent leur essor."* Leroy–Beaulieu, p. 166.

[2] *Ibid.,* p. 167.

[3] *Edit portant réglement pour le commerce des colonies françaises, Recueil Général,* xxi, p. 142; Malachy Postlethwayt, *Britain's Commercial Interest* (London, 1751), ii, pp. 22–47; Raynal, vii, p. 22; Postlethwayt's *Savary's Dictionary,* i, pp. 856–858.

[4] Postlethwayt, *Britain's Commercial Interest,* ii, p. 22.

[5] *Ibid.,* p. 32; Leroy-Beaulieu, p. 167.

keep pace with the rapid development of New York, or of New England. Thus Governor Bernard of Massachusetts, admits that while in 1733 the British West Indies might possibly have taken off the surplus products of the American colonies, in 1763 American commerce had doubled, and the trade with the foreign islands was therefore absolutely essential, and was worthy of encouragement.[1]

From and after 1717 the British West Indies gradually lost their hold on all markets except that of England. French sugars drove English sugars out of the markets of the European continent and competed very seriously with them in the colonies.[2] The price of French sugars gradually declined. Thus Postlethwayt admits it to be a fact that the French in the West Indies had sold their sugars from thirty to forty per cent. cheaper than the English.[3] Various causes were assigned for this difference in price. The inhabitants of Barbadoes claimed that their land was so exhausted that it required three negroes to raise as much sugar, as was formerly raised by one.[4] On the other hand it was said that, while the French and Dutch were frugal, the English were luxurious and extravagant. Gee says that both statements were true. "The Island of Barbadoes," he writes, "is very much worn out, and does not afford the Quantity of Sugars as heretofore, and yet the Planters live in great splendor, and at vast Expence, while the French, under the Remembrance of their Poverty on their first settlement of Hispaniola, continue to live very frugally, and by their Labour, Industry and Fertili y of their Soil, are able to undersell us."[5]

---

[1] *Select Letters*, pp. 6, 7; *cf.* Pownall, *The Administration of the Colonies* (London, 1768), p. 6.

[2] Postlethwayt, *The Importance of the African Expedition* (London, 1758), pp. 38, 39.

[3] *Commercial Interest*, i, p. 494.   [4] Macpherson, iii pp. 176, 177.

[5] Gee., p. 45; *cf.* Raynal, vii, p. 316.

As French sugar was cheaper, it was but natural that the Northern colonies should purchase it in preference to English sugar. In addition, another cause contributed to lower the price of French molasses. Brandy was an important French product, and to protect it from the competition of any other liquor, the importation of rum into France was prohibited.[1] This, therefore, made French molasses worthless unless a market were found for it elsewhere. This market was found in the Northern colonies, for molasses was the principal commodity that these colonies sought for in the West India trade. But the English islands produced little molasses, and it was said that at the time of peace of Paris Jamaica was the only one of the English islands that produced this article, and that the amount produced was by no means sufficient for the demand of the continental colonies.[2] Most naturally the New Englander, or New Yorker, preferred to purchase his rum and molasses in the cheapest markets. American vessels occasionally returned from Jamaica without cargoes, because the rum and molasses there were so dear.[3]

It will be remembered that the decline of the English islands, viewed as a unit, was only relative, that is, they did not increase so rapidly as their neighbors. Moreover, while the English had lost some markets, the demand for sugar in England had increased enormously. But at the same time it was claimed that the great prosperity of the French islands was mainly due to their trade with the Northern colonies.[4]

Against this trade of the Middle and New England colonies with the foreign West Indies the English islands protested

[1] Postlethwayt's *Commercial Interest*, i, p. 491.

[2] *Rhode Island Colonial Records*, vi, p. 382.

[3] Macpherson, iii, p. 165. Parkman tells us of the unsuccessful attempt of Canada to supply the French West Indies with provisions. *Old Régime*, p. 292.

[4] Campbell, *Sugar Trade*, p. 14.

most vigorously.   Already in 1715 the English sugar colonies complained of New England's vast trade with the Dutch
colony of Surinam.   The Dutch, they said, were supplied
with horses, fish and provisions by the New Englanders, who
took molasses in exchange and made rum out of it.[1]

In 1731 the planters of the British sugar colonies sent
numerous petitions to England.[2]   Barbadoes said that the
French and Dutch supplied the Northern colonies with rum
and molasses, and that while the other islands advanced,
those of England declined.[3]   Thus the attention of parliament was called to the question.   The same year a bill
passed the House of Commons, providing that no sugar,
rum, or molasses from the plantations of foreign nations
should be imported into Great Britain, Ireland, or any of the
American colonies, under pain of forfeiture.[4]   And since the
great number of horses, and the large quantity of lumber exported from the continental colonies to the foreign sugar
islands had enabled these islands the more easily to carry on
their sugar plantations, the exportation of these commodities
to the foreign colonies was thereafter to be forbidden.[5]

In support of the bill it was urged that the trade carried
on by the Northern colonies since 1715 was both detrimental
to the British sugar colonies, and also afforded the continental colonies an opportunity to supply themselves with French
manufactures.[6]   While formerly the English islands paid in
commodities for everything they purchased from the continental colonies, now they paid for one-half in money.   Their
money was then carried to the French islands. where rum
and molasses were obtained in exchange for it.[7]   Whereas

---

[1] Macpherson, iii, p. 49; p. 171; *cf.* Anderson, iii, p. 291; pp. 434, 435.

[2] Ashley, *Memoirs and Considerations*, part i, p. 1.   [3] *Ibid*, pp. 3-5.

[4] Macpherson, iii, pp. 171, 172; Anderson, iii, p. 433.

[5] *Ibid.*, p. 172; Anderson, iii, p. 434.

[6] *Ibid.*   [7] *Ibid.*, p. 173; Anderson, iii, 435.

formerly the English supplied France, Holland, Germany and Italy with sugar, now, on account of this trade, they were confined to the home consumption of Great Britain.[1]

The case of the continental colonies was argued with more ability and with more reason. They urged that "as all the sugar, rum, and molasses, of our sugar isles are taken off at high prices by Great Britain and the Northern colonies, it would be very impolitic to obstruct the latter from taking molasses, and even rum, from the French islands for the supply of their Indian trade, and much more of their fisheries; seeing our own sugar Colonies are unable to supply the great quantity of molasses which those two trades demand; more especially as from the French islands they receive in payment silver and cacao, as well as melasses (but seldom sugar or rum), which silver comes ultimately to Great Britain to pay for the balance of trade: and the northern colonies distill the molasses into rum for the above purposes."[2] They claimed that the prosperity of the Dutch and French was due on the one hand to their frugality and industry, and, on the other hand, to the luxury and extravagance of the English and the consequent high price of their sugar.[3] And they justly added, that only by this trade were they able to pay for the vast quantity of English manufactures consumed.[4]

The dispute was not settled at this time; the House of Lords would not pass the bill.[5] Two years later, however, the famous "Molasses Act" was passed. The act is entitled "for the better securing and encouraging the trade of his Majesty's sugar colonies in America." The prohibitions of the former bill were here veiled by practically prohibitory duties. After December 25th, 1733, the following duties

[1] Macpherson, iii, p. 174. [2] *Ibid.*, p. 175; Anderson, iii, pp. 436, 437.

[3] Macpherson, iii, p. 175. [4] *Ibid.*, p. 177.

[5] *Ibid.*, p. 171; Anderson, iii, p. 433; *The Rights of the British Colonies* (London, 1769), p. 7.

were to be paid on rum, *etc.*, made in the foreign plantations and imported into the British colonies in America:

Rum and spirits....................................... . ... 9 d. per gallon.
Molasses and syrup.. 6 d. per gallon.
Sugar .... 5 sh. per cwt.

At the same time certain privileges were given to English sugars, as regards the Irish trade,[1] and as regards drawbacks.[2]

Although in the form of an act granting revenue, this law operated simply as a regulation of commerce, for the duties on molasses were so high as to be prohibitory.[3] As stated above, any act which limited the trade between the Northern colonies and the West Indies was in direct contradiction to the policy of restricting manufactures in the colonies. "It is evident," writes the celebrated lawyer, John Dickinson, "that if our taking off and paying for her manufactures is beneficial to Great Britain, the channels by which we acquire money for that purpose, ought to be industriously kept open and uninterrupted."[4] To obey both measures would have meant at least stagnation, if not self-destruction. There could be no doubt as to which acts would be violated. Manufactures in very young settlements can at best thrive only under very artificial conditions. Such conditions, it is true, existed, in a measure, in the colonies, for the regulations of Charles II., the duties on corn, and the prohibitions to import salt provisions, had produced them. But the effect of the Corn Laws was mitigated by the West India trade, and so long as the colonies had an unrestricted outlet for their agricultural products and the poorer qualities of fish, they would continue to consume English manufactures. For, as

[1] 6 Geo. III., c. 13, § iv.   [2] *Ibid.,* § ix.

[3] "Mr. Otis asserted this to be a revenue law; a taxation law; an unconstitutional law; a law subversive of every end of society and government; it was null an void." Adams, *Works,* x, p. 348.

[4] *Political Writings* of John Dickinson, i, p. 51.

Mr. Merivale so aptly says, "the prohibition to manufacture for themselves was a prohibition to do that which, on a large scale, nature itself had forbidden them to do, by calling them to the more profitable occupation of agriculture."[1]   Thus, if the Molasses Act were enforced, agriculture and the fisheries of the Northern colonies must decline, and they would be forced to manufacture for themselves.   As it was, the colonists most naturally disregarded that act by disobedience to which they would gain the most.   The Molasses Act remained practically a dead letter.   Economically it was a gross mistake, and was the outcome of the spirit of paternalism shown toward the English colonies in the West Indies.

From the political standpoint, the act was also a blunder. The open and necessary disregard of law conduced, in some degree, to that contempt for acts of parliament which manifested itself in New England during the revolutionary epoch. As the biographer of Vane says, "the demoralization came to pass which always results when a community, even with good reason, is full of law-breakers."[2]

[1] Merivale, *Lectures on Colonies*, ii, p. 93.

[2] Hosmer, *Anglo-Saxon Freedom*, pp. 200, 201; Hosmer, *Samuel Adams*, p. 29; *cf.* also Arthur Young, *A Tour in Ireland* (Dublin, 1780), p. xiv.

CHAPTER VII. THE ADMINISTRATION OF THE ACTS.

§ 1. *Officials Entrusted with the Execution of the Acts.*
By an Order in Council of July 4th, 1660, the Lord Chamberlain, the Earl of Southampton, Sir Anthony Ashley Cooper and others, were appointed to meet and sit as a committee to receive, hear, and examine memorials respecting the plantations in America.[1] In November of the same year, a standing council of trade was appointed, to take into consideration in what manner the trade and navigation of England might be encouraged, regulated and improved.[2] At the head of this body was the celebrated historian and statesman, Edward Hyde, Lord Clarendon.[3] A few weeks later a standing council for foreign plantations was appointed by the king, and at its head the great Chancellor was again placed.[4] This body was to take into consideration the present and future state and condition of the colonies.[5] The king likewise instructed them to inquire about the " severall growths and comodities of every shipp tradeing there and its ladeing and whither consigned and what the proceeds of that place have been in the late years."[6] The council was also to see to it that the Navigation Act which had just been passed was strictly executed.[7] And lastly they were required and empowered to advise, order, and dispose of all matters relating to the good government, improvement, and management of the colonies and that with the utmost skill and prudence.[8]

[1] *New York Colonial Documents*, iii, p. xiii, p. 30; Chalmers, *Opinions of Eminent Lawyers*, p. vii.

[2] *Ibid.*, iii, p. xiii; pp. 30–32.　[3] *Ibid.*, iii, p. 31.　[4] *Ibid.*, iii, p. xiii; pp. 32–34.

[5] *Ibid.*, iii, p. 34.　　[6] *Ibid.*, iii, p. 35.　　[7] *Ibid.*　　[8] *Ibid.*, p. 36.

In 1672 Charles II. made Anthony, Earl of Shaftesbury, and others, a council for all matters concerning trade and foreign plantations.[1] Two years later this council was dissolved, and by an order in council of March 12th, 1675, all matters relating to trade and plantations were referred to a committee of the Privy Council.[2] Throughout the reign of James II., and up to 1696 in the reign of William III., similar committees of the Privy Council attended to colonial affairs.[3]

In May, 1696, a permanent body was constituted, the famous Board of Trade and Plantations. The members were to be the Keeper of the Great Seal or Chancellor, the President of the Privy Council, the Keeper of the Privy Seal, the Lord Treasurer, the Lord High Admiral, the principal Secretaries of State and the Chancellor of the Exchequer. In addition to these certain other members were appointed, among whom the most important were John Locke and John Pollexfen.[4] This board was required to examine into the general condition of England's foreign trade.[5] The commissioners were likewise required to inform themselves of the present condition of the colonies, both as to the administration of government and justice, and as to commerce. They were to devise means for securing the colonies, and rendering them useful to England.[6] In order to accomplish this purpose, the commissioners were to inquire whether such necessary commodities as naval stores could be produced in the colonies. They were to find out what industries, which might ultimately prove deleterious to England's prosperity, were springing up in the colonies.[7] Furthermore, the commissioners were empowered to examine the acts of the colonial legislatures which were sent to England for ap-

[1] New York Colonial Documents, iii, p. xiv.   [2] Ibid., pp. 229, 230.

[3] Ibid., iii, pp. xiv, xv.   [4] Ibid., iii, p. xv; iv, p. 146.   [5] Ibid.

[6] Ibid., iv, p. 147.   [7] Ibid., iv, p. 147.

probation, in order to see whether they contained anything harmful, either to England, or to the colonies.[1]   From time to time written reports of their proceedings were to be sent to the Privy Council.[2]

Of the high character of this body, a list of the more important among its members will furnish adequate testimony. At various periods Locke, Matthew Prior, Pulteney, Addison, Pitt, Grenville and Townshend, the most prominent men of their times, were members of it.[3]   In this Board of Trade colonial affairs were discussed, and here most of the policies, embodied later in parliamentary statutes, were adopted. Various means were employed for obtaining full information concerning colonial affairs.   Thus at one of its meetings, a list of all ships that had entered or cleared from a port in North Carolina was read.[4]   The colonial governors continually corresponded with the members of the Board, and kept them accurately informed as to the economic condition of the colonies.   Other officials and also private persons wrote to the board, requesting it to further some one industry, or to suppress another.   Occasionally elaborate memorials, dealing with the trade of all the colonies, were presented for the consideration of this body.

The legislatures of some of the colonies passed laws recognizing the validity of the navigation acts.   The assemblies of Virginia and Maryland recognized the collectors as legal officers, and distinguished between country dues and parliamentary customs.[5]   In Rhode Island the legislature passed an act enabling the governor to provide for the execution of the acts.[6]   In 1663 it was provided in Massachu-

---

[1] *New York Colonial Documents*, iv, p. 147.	[2] *Ibid.*, p. 148.

[3] *New York Colonial Records*, iii, pp. xv, xvi, xvii.

[4] *Colonial Records of North Carolina*, iii, p. 534.

[5] Chalmers, *Revolt*, i, p. 126.

[6] *Rhode Island Colonial Records*, iii, p. 437.

setts that the regulation in regard to the bonds of enumerated commodities should be executed.[1]   Two years later the court declared that the acts had for several years already been observed in Massachusetts.[2]   At the time of the troubles with Randolph it was maintained in Massachusetts that the king in parliament had no authority over them.[3]   In 1677 the general court ordered the acts to be executed, and claimed as an excuse for the former maladministration, that the will of the king had not been expressed to them before, either directly or through his ministers.[4]   The next year the court said that since the laws of England are bounded within the four seas, and since the colonists were not represented in parliament, the navigation acts had no legal validity in America.   Since, however, the king had desired the execution of these laws, the general court, in the previous year, had made provision for the same.   The court maintained that if it did not reënact a law of parliament that law had no validity in the colony, for otherwise the liberties of the subject would be infringed.[5]   A few years later the acts of 12 Charles II. and 15 Charles II. were ordered to be published in the market place, " by beate of drum."[6]

The colonial official under whose general supervision the execution of the acts of trade and navigation was placed, was the governor.   He had to take an oath that he would do his utmost to see that all these laws and regulations were

---

[1] *Massachusetts Colonial Records*, iv, 2, p. 73;   *Colonial Laws of Massachusetts*, (1672–1686), p. 139;   *Andros Tracts*, ii, p. 114.

[2] *Massachusetts Colonial Records*, iv, 2, p. 202;   p. 194.

[3] Adams, *Works*, iv, p. 111.

[4] *Massachusetts Colonial Records*, v, p. 155;   *cf. Colonial Laws of Massachusetts*, (1672–86), p. 258.

[5] *Massachusetts Colonial Records*, v, p. 200;   Adams, *Works*, iv, pp. 111, 112.

[6] *Massachusetts Colonial Records*, v, p. 337;   *Colonial Laws of Massachusetts*, (1672–1686), p. 289.

observed according to their true intent and meaning.[1] The
governors kept the Board of Trade informed as to the condition of affairs in the colonies. Their advice was frequently
sought and their propositions were often embodied in acts of
parliament. It depended mainly on this official, whether the
laws should be executed, or not. Thus, such an energetic
governor as the Earl of Bellomont would most naturally try
to suppress all illicit trade, and that he was successful to a
certain degree, we know from the fact that the trade of New
York declined during his tenure of office.[2]

Passing over such extraordinary officials as Edward Randolph, who, in 1675, was appointed " collector, surveyor, and
searcher " for all New England,[3] or as Colonel Quary, who
in 1703 was appointed surveyor general,[4] there are two other
officials who require consideration. These are the collector
of the customs, and the naval officer.[5] The collector, as the

[1] 12 Charles II., c. 18, p. ii. Mr. J. A. Doyle noticed a curious but characteristic
slip in this act of 1660 (*English in America, Puritan Colonies*, ii, p. 260). The
clause reads: " And all Governors .... and all who hereafter shall be made
Governors....by his Majesty, shall take the oath." 7 and 8 Wm. III., c. 22, p. iv,
remedied this. Mr. Doyle says that on account of this ambiguity the acts were so
far inapplicable to the New England colonies. In 1680, however, the court of
Massachusetts ordered that the governor take the oath as provided in the statute,
and that the same be administered by one of the Council. (*Massachusetts Colonial Records*, v, p. 262.) The report of the Lords Commissioners of Trade and
Plantations to the House of Commons of 1701, says: " The Governors in most of
these proprietary and charter governments have not taken the oaths required by
the acts of trade." *Mem. of Pennsylvania Historical Society*, ix, p. 379.

[2] *Massachusetts Historical Society Collections*, 3rd series, vii, p. 237.

[3] *Hutchinson Papers*, ii, p. 260 (Prince Society Publications). *Vide* Fiske, *Beginnings of New England*, p. 256; Doyle, *Puritan Colonies*, ii, 254; *Massachusetts
Historical Society Collections*, 3d Series, vii, p. 132.

[4] *Massachusetts Historical Society Proc.*, 2nd series, iv, p. 148. We find a *Sur-
veyor-general* in South Carolina appointed by the king. *Historical Collections of
South Carolina*, ii, p. 220. In some of the colonies there was a *Comptroller of the
Customs*. 3 Geo. II., c. 28.

[5] *Spotswood Letters*, i, p. 29 (Virginia Historical Society).

name implies, was authorized to collect whatever customs might arise under the acts. In case a vessel or its cargo was confiscated for violation of the navigation acts, he attended to the sale of the same.[1] He was appointed by the commissioners of the treasury or of the customs in England.[2] Although the governor had nothing to do with the appointment of this official, yet if the collector misbehaved and was negligent in his duties, the governor suspended him.[3]

The naval officer was entrusted with the duty of seeing to the execution of the provisions in the acts regarding bonds. He was to make entry of ships, inward or outward bound, to give clearances and certificates.[4] The power of appointing this official was vested in the governor.[5] The naval officers had however to give security to the commissioners of the customs in England for the faithful performance of their duty.[6] As the governors appointed them, so, if they saw fit, they could remove them.[7]

It was provided in the act of 1660[8] that ships violating navigation law might be prosecuted in any court of record.[9] According to an opinion delivered by Sir John Cooke, the king's advocate, in 1702: "the words of the act are general,

---

[1] *New York Colonial Documents*, iv, p. 1142; v, p. 232.

[2] 7 and 8 Will. III., c. 22, § xi. *Historical Collections of South Carolina*, ii, p. 221; *cf.* also *New York Colonial Documents*, iii, pp, 221, 222, 335, 336, 500–503; iv, pp. 335, 500. Before James became king he appointed this official in New York.

[3] *New York Colonial Documents*, iv, p. 321, 827, p. 1142.

[4] *Massachusetts Colonial Records*, v, p. 337; *Rhode Island Colonial Records*, iii, p. 110.

[5] 15 Charles II., c. 7, § viii; 7 and 8 Will. III. c. 22, § v; *Connecticut Colonial Records*, 1706–1716, p. 437; *New York Colonial Documents*, iv, p. 304, p. 316, p. 318; *Spotswood Letters*, i, p. 14.

[6] 7 and 8 Will. III., c. 22, § v; *New York Colonial Documents*, iv, p. 318, p. 603, p. 664.

[7] *Spotswood Letters*, i, p. 96.   [8] 12 Charles II., c. 18, § vi.

[9] Hammond, *Blackstone Commentaries*, iii, p. 24.

without a particular mention of England, or of the plantations, and included the Admiralty Courts of both places,
they being the King's courts, and consequently Courts of
Record."[1]   The other acts passed during the reign of Charles
II., although they hint at the jurisdiction of the admiralty
courts, do not explicitly provide for it.[2]   Thus, 22 and 23
Charles II., c. 26, says that prosecutions for a breach of the
navigation acts shall be tried in the court of the high admiral
of England, in any of the vice-admiralty courts, or in any court
of record in England.[3]   When the celebrated administrative
statute of 1696 was passed, explicit provision was made in
it for the jurisdiction of the admiralty courts in cases involv-
ing a breach of the acts of trade.[4]

In certain of the colonies there was little need of an admiralty court, as little illegal trade was carried on.   Thus we
are told that the admiralty court of Virginia did not try a
single case during the reigns of the last two Stuarts.[5]   In
Massachusetts different conditions prevailed.   At first there
was no regular admiralty court in this colony, but the other
courts acted as such when occasion demanded.[6]   In 1673 it
was provided in Massachusetts that all admiralty cases should
be determined by the Court of Assistants acting without a jury,
" unless the Court shall see cause to the contrary."[7]   That

---

[1] Forsyth, *Cases and Opinions on Constitutional Law*, p. 91.

[2] Forsyth, pp. 91, 92.   [3] § xi.

[4] 7 and 8 Will. III., c. 22, § vii.

[5] Hening, ii, p. 572.

[6] In 1673 the general court refused to consider the case of a ship because the
illegal acts had been committed outside of its jurisdiction, and referred the case to
the King's Court of Admiralty. *Massachusetts Colonial Records*, iv. 2, pp. 573, 574.

[7] *Massachusetts Colonial Records*, iv, 2, p. 575; *cf.* Washburn, *Judicial History
of Massachusetts*, pp. 30, 68, 172.   Yet in 1676 the general court acted as the admiralty court. *Massachusetts Colonial Records*, v, p. 131.   In 1678 Andros said
about New York : " The Court of Admiralty hath been by speciall commission or
by the Court of Mayor or Aldermen att New Yorke."

this court often acted with a jury, we know from the fact that the juries would not convict those whom Randolph accused.[1]

One step in the organization of the colonial administration by William III. was the appointing of regular admiralty courts in the colonies.[2] Acting on the advice of Locke, admiralty courts were instituted in most of the colonies.[3] The judges and officers received their commission from the Lord High Admiral, but in reality they were appointed by the Lords Commissioners of the Admiralty.[4] Appeals from these courts ran to the king in council, or rather to that portion of the Privy Council called "The Lords Commissioners for hearing Appeals from the Plantations in America."[5]

As the salaries of many of the above-mentioned officials were obtained from fees and a certain percentage of the confiscated commodities, or were paid by the colonies, the administrative expenses incurred by the home goverment were not very great. Yet they tended to exceed the receipts. According to Lecky, "Grenville found on examination that the whole revenue derived by England from the customhouses in America amounted to between 1,000l. and 2,000l. a year; that for the purpose of collecting this revenue the English Exchequer paid annually between 7,000l. and 8,000l."[6]

§ 2. *Illegal Trade and Smuggling.* In the history of the

[1] *Andros Tracts*, ii, p. 128: "It's true Mr. Randolph seized and prosecuted severall vessels and goods for irregular trading: but upon the tryall (as we understood) his proofes were so very defective that the Jurys could not find for his Maty."

[2] Washburn, p. 172; Chalmers, *Revolt*, i, p. 275.

[3] Burnaby's *Travels*, p. 81; *New York Colonial Documents*, iv, pp. 828, 829.

[4] *Historical Collections of South Carolina*, ii, p. 221; Washburn, p. 172; *Dinwiddie Papers*, i, p. 384.

[5] *Dinwiddie Papers*, i, p. 384; *Massachusetts Historical Society Proceedings* 2nd Series, V., p. 86; Burnaby, p. 102.

[6] *Grenville Papers*, ii, p. 114, quoted in Lecky, ii, p. 333.

execution of the acts, from the days of Charles II. to the accession of George III., we can in a general way distinguish three periods. Before 1696 the administrative machinery had not been well organized, and consequently the execution of the acts was lax, especially at the time when Randolph was sent to the colonies. In 1696 a new epoch opens. At this time the Board of Trade was established, a comprehensive administrative statute was passed, and courts of admiralty were established in the colonies. This period of strict administration lasted through the reigns of William and Anne and until the Walpole era. According to Walpole's views colonial commerce should be encouraged, for colonial prosperity must ultimately redound to the benefit of England by increasing the demand for her products. Walpole left the care of colonial affairs to the Duke of Newcastle, whose ignorance of American geography has became proverbial. The Duke treated the colonies with what has been termed salutary neglect,[1] keeping his closet full of unopened dispatches from American governors.[2] This period of lax administration lasted until the Seven Years War, when a radical change was introduced into the policy.

Any attempt to describe the illicit trade of the colonies must be preceded by a succinct account of the amount of smuggling in England, for such an account will show that the Englishman, as well as the colonist, was forced into illegal acts both by injudicious taxes, and by law administrative regulations. Of the England of William III. Macaulay writes, "whole fleets of boats with illicit cargoes had been passing and repassing between Kent and Picardy. The loading and unloading had taken place sometimes in Romney Marsh, sometimes on the beach under the cliff, between Dover and Folkstone. All the inhabitants of the southeastern coast were in the plot. It was a common saying among

---

[1] Burke, *Speeches* (ed. 1816), i, p. 285.   [2] John Morley, *Walpole*, pp. 168, 169.

them, that, if a gallows were set up every quarter of a mile along the coast, the trade would still go on briskly." This was the condition as regards the illegal importation of French silks. Pitt calculated a century later that " about thirteen million pounds' weight of tea were consumed every year in England, while only five millions and a half were sold by the East India Company, so that the illicit trade in this article was more than the legal trade.[1] According to Earl Stanhope this trade " had been reduced to a regular system; forty thousand persons by sea and by land were said to be engaged in it; and the large capital requisite for their operations came, as was believed, from gentlemen of rank and character in London. Ships—some of 300 tons burden—lay out at sea and dealt out their cargoes of tea to small colliers and barges, by which they were landed at different places along the coast, where bands of armed men were stationed to receive and protect them."[2]

When such conditions prevailed in England, it is by no means surprising that in the colonies, where the trade regulations were more stringent, and where the administration of them was much more difficult,[3] conditions essentially the same or even worse prevailed.

As in institutional and economic development, so in the question of contraband trade, we can draw a sharp line of demarcation between the Southern colonies, and the Middle and Northern colonies. In the Southern colonies little illicit trade was carried on. Thus Governor Berkeley, of Virginia, complains: "We are most obedient to all laws, whilst the New England men break through them and trade to any place that their interest leads them to."[4] Later it was said of South Carolina: "No country in this part of the world hath

---

[1] Stanhope, *Pitt*, i, p. 215.

[2] *Ibid.*, pp. 215, 216.

[3] *Dinwiddie Papers*, i, p. 380.

[4] Chalmers, *Political Annals*, p. 128.

less illegal trade than South Carolina." [1]   This difference was a natural one, for the Southerner had little temptation to evade the laws.   He found in England an eager market for his tobacco, rice, and naval stores.   Nor was there much inducement to send these commodities elsewhere, for tobacco drew the whole duty back on reëxportation, rice could be sent directly to countries South of Cape Finisterre, and naval stores received bounties in England.   In England also the Southerner could purchase most easily and cheaply the commodities he desired, such as woolens and other manufactures.

There were, however, two branches of illegal trade in which the Southerner indulged.   A statute of Charles II. imposed duties on the enumerated commodities when transported from one colony to another. [2]   The duty of one penny per pound on tobacco was the clause especially affecting the continental colonies.   In violation of this statute, tobacco was continually imported by the Northern from the Southern colonies without paying any duties. [3]   Yet the quantity so imported was small, since it was used mainly in home consumption.   The other contraband trade was that with the West Indies.   This trade was a natural one, as the West Indies produced certain necessaries of life which could be readily purchased for tobacco, rice, lumber, or wheat. [4]   Thus Governor Spotswood repeatedly complains of the illicit trade of Virginia with St. Thomas and with the Dutch island Curaçoa. [5]   This was, however, during the war of the Spanish

---

[1] *Historical Collections of South Carolina*, ii, p. 232; *cf. New York Colonial Documents*, iv, p. 79.

[2] *Cf.* above, p. 39.

[3] *Cf.* Hawks, *History of North Carolina*, ii, p. 235; *Massachusetts Historical Society Proceedings*, 2nd series, iv, p. 150; *New York Colonial Documents*, v, pp. 30–33.

[4] *Dinwiddie Papers*, i, p. 386; *Spotswood Letters*, i, p. 10, 15.

[5] *Spotswood Letters*, i, pp. 18, 87.

succession, when exceptional circumstances prevailed, and when, since the administration was necessarily lax, much illicit trade was carried on in all the colonies.[1]   In general we may say that the illegal trade of the Southern colonies was insignificant in comparison with that of the other colonies.

The reasons for this difference are not hard to find.   The Northerner, producing few commodities for which he could find a market in England, was forced to enter into commercial relations with other countries.   He was tempted, and in a measure forced, to buy commodities in these countries, since the mercantile system prevailed generally throughout Europe.   Thus, when he sold his fish or his flour to the foreign West Indies, he had to take molasses in return, and was sorely tempted to take some French manufactures.   For in those days, when no cable existed and the banking system was not fully developed, it was a very inconvenient method of business to sell in one market and to buy in another.

The illicit trade of the Northern colonies centred about Boston, Philadelphia and New York.   The coast near these cities was especially adapted for smuggling.   Goods were landed at Cape Ann, and conveyed into Boston into small wooden boats.[2]   Long Island and its vicinity was especially noteworthy as the resort of contraband traders,[3] and fully deserved the epithet that Edmund Burke bestows upon the Isle of Man, "the very citadel of smuggling."[4]

Keeping this distinction before our minds, we can now discuss the subject of the execution of the acts, both those acts restricting certain industries, and those requiring that the

[1] Chalmers, *Revolt*, i, p. 269.   [2] *New York Colonial Documents*, iv, p. 792.

[3] *Ibid.*, iv, p. 591; *Massachusetts Historical Society Proceedings*, 2nd series, iv, p. 149.

[4] Burke, "American Taxation," in *Speeches* (ed. 1816), i, p. 197.

economic development should follow certain prescribed grooves. The policy of restricting manufactures in the colonies was in general most successful. On the whole, the three acts aimed against woolen, hat and iron[1] industries were generally obeyed. The success of this policy is easily explained, for extensive manufactures in such young countries as the colonies, can only be due to a *pis-aller.*[2] In the Southern colonies even the most rudimentary forms of manufactures were absent, while in the Northern colonies there were many artisans, but manufactures were, as a rule, confined to the household. The ship-building industry of Pennsylvania and New England forms an exception to this general rule. What Professor Ashley says of England in the fourteenth century, can, with equal applicability, be said of the colonies in 1756. "Such manufactures as it possessed were entirely for consumption within the land; and for goods of the finer qualities it was dependent on importation from abroad."[3] The only exports were the tobacco and rice of the Southern colonies, the more varied agricultural products of the Middle colonies, and the fish of New England.

Equally well executed were those statutes of Charles II. which gave a monopoly of the carrying trade to and from the colonies to English shipping. This was most natural, for the temptations to violate them were altogether lacking. Writes Benjamin Franklin, " the Navigation Act was acceptable to us, since we wished to employ our own ships in preference to foreigners, and had no desire to see foreign ships enter our ports."[4]

[1] *New York Colonial Documents,* vi, p. 604; *Documentary History of New York,* i, pp. 729, 730, 735; Weeden, p. 734; Bishop, i, p. 625; *Parliamentary History,* xvi, p. 151; Ford, *Report of 1791,* p. 30.

[2] Ramsay, *History of the American Revolution* (London, 1793), i, p. 43.

[3] Ashley, *Economic History,* i, 1, pp. 5, 6.

[4] *Works,* edited by Sparks, v, pp. 15, 16.

Those provisions which regulated the importation of European goods into the colonies were not so well executed. The trade carried on by the Northern colonies with Newfoundland afforded many opportunities for violating the laws of trade. Under the pretense of carrying on a trade in fish, wines, brandies, and other European goods were, contrary to law, imported thence directly into the colonies.[1] In the instructions to Governor Andros (1686-7) Newfoundland is described as "a magazine of all sorts of goods brought thither directly from France, Holland, Scotland, Ireland and other places."[2]

The monopoly of trade beyond the Cape of Good Hope, which had been granted to the East India Company,[3] was frequently infringed by the colonists. Lord Bellomont continually complains of their trade with Madagascar.[4] They traded with the pirates of this region, and bought from them great quantities of East India goods.[5] On the 25th of May 1689, Bellomont wrote, "I am informed there hath been a most lycencious Trade with Pyrats, Scotland and Curaçoa, and the Collector here Mr. Chidley Brook is most extremely backward in the discharge of his duty."[6] This trade however soon declined.[7]

With Scotland[8] before the Act of Union, and with Ireland, there was always considerable illicit trade. Many ships, carrying enumerated commodities such as tobacco,[9] landed at some Irish port, and claimed as excuse the stress of

[1] New York Colonial Documents, iii, pp. 407, 493; Massachusetts Historical Society Collections, 3rd series, vii, p. 174; New York Colonial Documents, iv, p. 792; Charles Pedley, The History of Newfoundland, pp. 99, 102.

[2] Massachusetts Historical Society Collections, 3rd series, vii, p. 174.

[3] Reeves, A History of the Laws of Shipping and Navigation (Dublin, 1792), pp. 119-121.

[4] New York Colonial Documents, iv, p. 304.

[5] Ibid.; also ibid. pp. 299, 319, 323.   [6] Ibid., iv, pp. 317, 318.

[7] Ibid., iv, p. 792.   [8] Ibid., iv, pp. 317, 318.   [9] Ibid., iv, p. 301.

weather.[1] The enumerated commodities were occasionally sent to the Azores and Madeiras, whence the colonists were allowed to import some commodities directly.[2]

New England carried on a most extensive trade in fish with Portugal and Spain, and most naturally imported other goods besides money and salt.[3] To prevent this illicit trade Gee, wanted a regulation that all ships trading with those countries should touch at some English port before returning to the colonies.[4] One of the two indulgences allowed in the execution of the laws of trade was, according to Sir Francis Bernard, the permission accorded to ships carrying fish to Portugal, to return thence with wines and fruits in small quantities.[5] Some fish was likewise sent to Toulon and Marseilles, and French manufactures were imported directly thence.[6] Likewise we find Barcelona handkerchiefs being sold in the colonies.[7] References are continually made to the temptations to which this trade with Southern Europe[8] exposed the New Englanders.[9]

It was in the West India trade, especially, that the laws were disregarded. As we have shown above, the Molasses Act of 1733 could not be executed, unless the colonists were willing to retrograde. Many ingenious methods were resorted to in order to circumvent the law. Many merchants left Jamaica with empty casks, having obtained there false clearances from the custom house for sugar or molasses sup-

---

[1] 7 and 8 Will. III., c. 22.

[2] *Massachusetts Historical Society Proceedings*, 2d series. iv, pp. 154, 155.

[3] Weeden, p. 663.   [4] Gee, *Trade*, chapter xxv, pp. 48–53.

[5] Sir Francis Bernard, *Select Letters* (London, 1774), p. 2; letter ii.

[6] Weeden, p. 663.   [7] *Ibid.*, p. 612.

[8] In 1721 it was said, " it is easy to import all sorts of goods from the Streights, France and Spain, although prohibited." Weeden, p. 556.

[9] *New York Colonial Documents*, iv, pp. 791, 792; *Massachusetts Historical Society Proceedings*, 2nd series, iv, p. 153; *Letter* (London, 1720), p. 37.

posed to be in these casks.   In the French islands the casks
were filled.   Since, however, they had the clearances from
Jamaica, the merchants escaped paying the heavy duties imposed by the Molasses Act.[1]   Although some revenue was
collected from these duties,[2] the Molasses Act was practically a dead letter.[3]   As much foreign molasses was imported
after as before 1733.[4]   This was the chief illegal trade of the
Middle and Northern colonies, and afforded many opportunities for importing French manufactures into those colonies.[5]

We occasionally find governors and collectors conniving
at the various branches of contraband trade.   Governor
Fletcher of New York was charged with malfeasance, and
with connivance at the violation of the laws of trade.[6]   The
Earl of Bellomont continually complained of the criminal
negligence of the New York collectors.[7]   Colonel Quary
made similar complaints against a New England collector.[8]
There was, however, a strong social pressure preventing the
officials from executing certain of the laws.   In an obituary
of a collector of the customs in New England who died about
1733, it was said, " with much humanity (he) took pleasure
in directing Masters of Vessels how they ought to avoid the
Breach of the Acts of Trade."[9]   In 1719 Caleb Heathcote
wrote from Rhode Island, " and 'tis very wonderful to me,
who am thoroughly acquainted with the temper of the peo-

---

[1] Long, *Jamaica*, i, p. 539; Macpherson, iii, p. 403 n.

[2] Hutchinson, *History of Massachusetts*, iii.   [3] Bernard, *Select Letters*, Letter ii.

[4] Ashley, *Considerations*, part i, p. 39.   [5] Weeden, pp. 557, 558.

[6] Roberts, *New York*, p. 222; *New York Colonial Documents*, iv, p. 433; *cf.*
also *Dinwiddie Papers*, ii, pp. 679, 680.

[7] *New York Colonial Documents*, vol. iv, p. 30; *Massachusetts Historical Society
Proceedings*, 2nd series, iv, p. 150.

[8] *Massachusetts Historical Society Proceedings*, 2nd series, iv, p. 150.

[9] Weeden, p. 557.

ple, that none of his Majesty's officers of the customs have
been mobbed, and torn in pieces by the rabble, and of which
some of them have very narrowly escaped."[1]

These are the most important branches of illegal trade. It
will be necessary now to determine what proportion this
bore to the legal trade, and in what degree it vitiated
the main purposes of the colonial system. This question is
a most difficult one to answer, as difficult as it would be
nowadays, using the daily editorials, to give an adequate and
just account of the degree of corruption in our legislative
bodies. For most of our evidence is *ex parte*. From the
reports of Quary much is learned about contraband trade,
yet Quary is by no means trustworthy. Being a purely
royal official, he had no checks to keep him from exaggeration. Then, besides this, a contemporary, William Penn,
speaks of "Quary's and his few venomous adherents' proceedings,"[2] and again later he says, "Quary or any of his
rude and ungrateful gang."[3] Although Penn had every
reason to be prejudiced against Quary, his opinion seems to
be the correct one.[4] That Quary was inclined to exaggerate
the misdoings of any but a royal colony is undoubtedly true.[5]
The impartiality of Randolph's representations is open to
even graver doubts. Taking into consideration the untrust-
worthy character of such evidence, and the absence of adequate statistics, the impossibility of giving anything but an
approximate answer to this question will be self-evident. A
few quotations from contemporary writers will, however,
throw a good deal of light on this subject.

In 1675, in the days of Edward Randolph, it was said that
vessels from every European country, as well from France

---

[1] *Rhode Island Colonial Records*, iv, p. 259.

[2] *Memoirs of the Historical Society of Pennsylvania*, ix, p. 271.   [3] *Ibid.*, p. 272

[4] *Cf. Massachusetts Historical Society Proceedings*, 2nd series, iv, p. 147.

[5] *Cf. Massachusetts Historical Society Collections*, 3rd series, vii, p. 229.

and Spain as from Holland and Italy, were seen in Boston harbor.[1]   On the other hand, the governor of Massachusetts said, in 1679, "that it was impossible to prevent some vessels going to France and Holland, the owners of which paid the duties in the colony; but that it had never traded irregularly for more than five thousand pounds a year."[2]   In corroboration of this, Simon Bradstreet wrote from Boston in 1680, "and that we violate all the acts of trade and navigation &c. whereby his ma'tie is damaged in his Customs to the value of 100,000 £ yearly, and the Kingdom much more, when as by the strictest inquyry that I can make of merchants, unconcerned and others, there hath never been 5000 £ irregularly traded by the merchants of this place a yeare."[3]

Andros made a most moderate, and probably accurate, statement when he declared " the acts of trade and navigation are sayed and are generally believed not to be obseryed in the collonyes as they ought."[4]   Mather takes an entirely different standpoint.   "And this again," he writes, " forces us to mention another matter in which that people has been sadly wronged; that is *their breaking the Acts of Navigation.*   We do then Affirm that the Government there and the whole body of the people would rejoice in the severest Execution of those Acts, and lend their utmost help thereunto.   There are but a few particular persons that have Transgressed in the forbidden Trade."[5]

The letters of the Earl of Bellomont, governor in New York, who tried about 1700 to enforce order in that colony, are full of references to illicit trade.   According to him " the carelessness and corruption of the officers of the revenue and

[1] Chalmers, *Political Annals*, pp. 400, 433.   [2] *Ibid.*, p. 408.

[3] *Massachusetts Historical Society Collections*, 3rd series, viii, p. 331.

[4] *Andros Tracts.* i, p. xx, p. 41; *New York Colonial Documents*, iii, pp. 260–265.

[5] *Andros Tracts*, ii, 57.

customes have been so great for some yeares past that although the Trade of this place hath been four times as much
as formerly and the City greatly enlarged and enriched, yet
his Majtys revenue arising from the Customes, hath decreased the one half from what it was ten years since; and
the Merchants here have been so used to unlawful trade that
they were almost ready to mutiny on some seizures I caused
to be made."[1]   In a later letter he added, "but the observ-
ance of the laws of trade was so great a Novelty that it gave
as great discontent as if it had been an infringement of their
Charter."[2]

Colonel Quary represented that the laws were systematically violated.   "I did design," he wrote in 1703, "to have
given to your Lordshipps, the History of Connecticut; but
on a nice enquiry, into the state of that place, I found the
roguery and villainy of that Province, both in relation to
Government and Trade is enough to fill a volume."[3]   Bellomont's policy in New York was partially successful, for in
1708 Lord Cornbury wrote, "that there has been a great
deal of illegal trade carried on in this Province formerly is
undoubtedly true.   I hope it has not been so bad of late years,
but yet I know there has been illegal Trade carried on between New England, Connecticut and the East End of Long
Island."[4]

The opinion of Burke on this matter as expressed in his
celebrated speech on American Taxation seems to me most
judicious.   "I know, Sir," he exclaimed, "that great and not

---

[1] *New York Colonial Documents*, iv, p. 303.   See also *ibid.*, p. 461.

[2] *Ibid.*, iv, p. 319.   See also *ibid.*, p. 516.

[3] *Massachusetts Historical Society Collections*, 3rd series, vii, p. 240.   See the two
other reports of Quary, the one in *Massachusetts Historical Society Proceedings*,
2nd series, iv, p. 148, the other in *New York Colonial Documents*, v, p. 30.   See
also Saunders, *Colonial Records of North Carolina*, i, p. 536; i, p. 540.

[4] *New York Colonial Documents*, v, p. 58.

unsuccessful pains have been taken to inflame our minds by an outcry, in this house and out of it, that in America the act of navigation neither is, or ever was obeyed. But if you take the colonies through, I affirm, that its authority never was disputed; that it was no where disputed for any length of time; and on the whole, that it was well observed. Wherever the act pressed hard, many individuals indeed evaded it."[1] What Burke meant is that the main purposes of the English colonial system were attained, while in some minor details the acts were systematically violated.[2]

In the main the colonies consumed English and not French manufactures; few goods were imported directly from the European continent. Thus even Lord Bellomont says, " I have watched the ships trading between this place and Holland, as nicely as I have been able, but never could find they traded thither and from thence hither without touching and clearing in England, as the law directs."[3] Likewise, in the main, the colonies sent the enumerated commodities to England. The truth of this is clearly apparent when we consider that by far the greater part of the rice and tobacco imported into England was reëxported to other countries. While on the other hand the attempt to aid the English West Indies by the Molasses Act was a dismal failure, since it was contrary to all economic forces. And the nullification

[1] Burke's *Speeches*, i, p. 203; *cf.* Ramsay's *American Revolution*, i, p. 44, " in severely checking a contraband, which was only the overflowing of an extensive fair trade."

[2] See Eben Greenough Scott's *The Development of Constitutional Liberty*, p. 198: " A great deal has been said of its being a dead letter, and there is no question of its being much and systematically evaded, particularly by the generation that resisted the Stamp Act; but the constant reference to it here and abroad, the continued legislation respecting it by Parliament show clearly that it maintained its position effectively, and that, both in America and in England, it was regarded as the very foundation upon which colonial social life was built."

[3] *New York Colonial Documents*, iv, p. 792.

of this act was, from the English point of view, most fortu-
nate. [For had this act been executed the colonists would
have been forced to manufacture for themselves; and had extensive manufactures arisen in the colonies, the very founda-
tions of the colonial system would have been overturned.]

CHAPTER VIII. CONCLUSION.

§ 1. *Change in Policy from the Seven Years' War to the Continental Congress.* With the Peace of Paris the colonial period proper comes to an end. During the next twenty years those forces that tended toward the separation of England and the colonies had full sway. This period, from 1756 to 1776, must be regarded as transitional, as a period during which it was to be determined whether the colonies were sufficiently mature, not only to assert, but also to maintain their independence. As Professor Fisher of Yale says in his recently published sketch, the record of this period "may conveniently find a place in connection with the era of the Revolution, of which it was the prelude."[1]

Up to 1763 England acted consistently on a false, but historically justifiable, economic principle. She had developed a rounded colonial system, based on economic principles, and but slightly influenced by political considerations.[2] Up to this time the main interest in England's colonial system is economic. After 1763 the economic interest largely disappears, and the *raison d'être* of the acts passed after this date, appears only when studied in close relation with political events. Economic motives are subordinated to political principles. Thus English statesmen could not, on account of the remission of the duty in England, expect to increase the

---

[1] Fisher, *The Colonial Era*, p. vii.

[2] It is evident that we disagree radically with Weeden's views. " England had no colonial policy. Her colonies were accidents, politically considered. Their administration and regulation, political and economic, were controlled by the ex igencies of English contests with continental powers," p. 232.

revenue[1] by the small duty on tea imported into the colonies. But this duty was maintained because parliament wished to assert its right to impose such port duties. On the other hand, when acts were passed whose operation it was feared would prove grievous to the colonies, the trade laws were mitigated as palliatives. Thus at the time of the passage of the Stamp Act,[2] besides other changes,[3] bounties were offered on colonial lumber,[4] and the production of silk[5] and coffee[6] in the colonies was encouraged by changes in the duties. [As Grenville himself, in 1766, said: " Ungrateful people of America ! Bounties have been extended to them. When I had the honour of serving the crown, while you yourselves were loaded with an enormous debt, you have given bounties on their lumber, on their iron, their hemp, and many other articles. You have relaxed, in their favour, the Act of Navigation, that palladium of the British commerce."[7]

[And in the opposition of the colonists to such acts as the taxes of Charles Townshend, economic motives were again subordinated to political principles. The colonists did not care so much for the money which they would have to pay, as for the acknowledgment thereby of the right of Parliament to tax them.[8]

[1] Lecky, *History of England*, iii, pp. 402, 403. Opposition was also made to the colonial system on the ground of natural law. The following passage appeared in the " Boston Gazette" of April 29th, 1765 : " Whose natural right is infringed by the erection of an American windmill, or the occupation of a water mill on a man's own land, provided he does not flood his neighbors?....a colonist cannot make a button, a horseshoe, nor a hob-nail, but some sooty ironmonger or respectable button-maker of Britain shall bawl and squall that his honor's worship is most egregiously maltreated, injured, cheated, and robbed by the rascally American republicans." Frothingham, *The Rise of the Republic of the United States*, p. 122, note.

[2] 5 Geo. III., c. 12.   [3] *Ibid.*, c. 45, §§ xix, xxii, xxiii.   [4] *Ibid.*, c. 45.

[5] *Ibid.*, c. 29.   [6] *Ibid.*, c. 45, § xi.   [7] *Parliamentary History*, xvi, p. 102.

[8] *Cf.* Josiah Tucker, *Cui Bono ?* (Glocester, 1781), p. 20: " The great Griev-

At the close of the Seven Years' War two changes of special importance were made in England's colonial policy. A stricter execution of the laws of trade was determined upon,[1] and at the same time it was decided to raise a revenue in the colonies by means of the Molasses Act.   Many causes may be assigned for this change in policy.   The late war had doubled England's debt, and it seemed only just that those for whom it had been partly incurred, should help to bear the burden.[2]   In addition, during the war the colonies had occasionally acted most unpatriotically, supplying the French with provisions, and then justifying their conduct by sophisims.[3]   In the third place the increase of colonial territory made the work of protection more expensive, and to such statesmen as Grenville and Townshend there seemed no reason why the colonies should not contribute their quota for this purpose.

Thus, while the restrictive trade regulations were to be executed, by changing the purpose of one act, and by enacting others, a revenue was to be raised from the colonies.   Formerly trade had been only regulated, now it was to be regulated and taxed.   As Burke said in one of his celebrated speeches: "Whether you were right or wrong in establishing the colonies on the principle of commercial monopoly, rather than on that of revenue, is at this day a problem of

ance of the Colonies and their bitter Complaints against the Mother Country were, that they were not governed a la Monsr. Locke. For, to give them their Due, they hardly made an objection to any thing besides. They did not pretend to say that the Half-penny Tax on News Papers at first, or the Three-penny Duty on Teas afterwards were intolerable Burdens in themselves;—but all the Grievance was, that the Parliament of Great Britain, and not the Assemblies of America had legalized them, and ordered them to be collected."

[1] VI, Winsor, p. 11; Grey, *Appendix to Quincy's Reports*, p. 407.

[2] Lecky, *The Political Value of History*, pp. 38–40.

[3] Grey's *Appendix*, pp. 407, 408 n., 436; Lecky, iii, p. 329; Hildreth, ii, p. 498; cf. *Dinwiddie Papers*, ii, p. 49, 456, 498, 525, 596, 606, 618, 621, 665; *New York Colonial Documents*, vii, p. 225.

mere speculation. You cannot have both by the same authority. To join together the restraints of an universal internal and external monopoly, with an universal internal and external taxation, is an unnatural union; perfect uncompensated slavery. You have long since decided for yourself and them, and you and they have prospered exceedingly under that decision."[1] Governor Bernard's letters likewise show the confusion caused by this change of policy. The Molasses Act, he writes, "has been a stumbling-block to Custom-house officers; the question seems to be whether it should be an act of Prohibition or an act of Revenue."[2]

After the fall of Bute in 1763, the Grenville ministry came into power. One object of Grenville's colonial policy was to raise a revenue from the colonies for defraying the expense of protecting them. For his purpose there was only one available statute in existence, *viz.*, the Molasses Act. This act was in the form of a revenue bill, but the rates of duty in it had been purposely placed so high as to be prohibitory.[3] The agent of Massachusetts in England warned the assembly that, as the Molasses Act was going to expire, it would undoubtedly be reënacted with important alterations, such as reductions in the duties on molasses and sugar.[4] This prediction proved true, for in 1764 the celebrated Sugar Act was passed.[5] The purpose of this act, as was stated in the preamble, was to raise a revenue to pay the cost of securing and defending the colonies.[6]

---

[1] Burke, *Speeches*, i, p. 204; *cf.* Rogers, *Economic Interpretation of History*, p. 324.

[2] *Select Letters*, pp. 5. 6.   [3] Hutchinson, *History of Massachusetts*, iii, p. 108.

[4] *Ibid.*, p. 104.   [5] 4 Geo. III., c. 15.

[6] "But the grand manœuvre in that business of new regulating the colonies, was ths 15th act of the fourth of George III; which, besides containing several of the matters to which I have just alluded, opened a new principle, and here properly began the second period of the policy of this country with regard to the Colonies; by which the scheme of a regular plantation parliamentary revenue was adopted in

To obtain this revenue duties were laid on many commodities imported into the colonies. These commodities were sugar from the foreign plantations in America, foreign indigo, coffee from any place except Great Britain, Madeira wines imported directly, Portuguese and Spanish wines imported through Great Britain, and silks and other textiles from Great Britain.[1] Duties were imposed upon colonial coffee and pimento exported from America to any country but England.[2] Then the Molasses Act was made perpetual, and the duty was reduced from six pence per gallon to three pence,[3] as John Ashley had suggested in 1740.[4] The importation of foreign rum into the colonies was at the same time positively prohibited.[5]

To this act there was much opposition in the colonies. John Dickinson of Pennsylvania wrote an able pamphlet against it, in which he showed that the West India trade was absolutely essential, if the colonists had to buy their manufactures in England.[6] In Massachusetts opposition was made to the principle of parliamentary taxation,[7] and it was also asserted that this act would destroy the New England fisheries.[8]

theory, and settled in practice. A revenue not substituted in the place of, but superadded to, a monopoly; which monopoly was enforced at the same time, with additional strictness, and the execution put into military hands." Burke, *Speeches*, i, p. 208.

[1] 4 Geo. III., c. 15, § 1.   [2] *Ibid.*, § ii.   [3] *Ibid.*, § iv, § v.

[4] Ashley, *Considerations and Memoirs*, p. 42; *cf.* Hutchinson's *Massachusetts*, p. 108.   [5] § xviii.

[6] " *The Late Regulations respecting the British Colonies on the Continent of America considered*," in Dickinson's *Political Writings*, Vol. I; *cf.* Stillé's *John Dickinson*, p. 68.

[7] Hutchinson's *Massachusetts*, iii, p. 106.

[8] "Our pickled fish wholly, and a great part of the cod fish, are fit only for the West India market. The British Islands cannot take off one-third of the quantity caught; the other two-thirds must be lost or sent to the foreign plantations, where molasses are given in exchange. The duty on this article will greatly diminish its importation hither, and being the only article allowed to be given in exchange for

This opposition and the feeling engendered by the Stamp Act in the colonies induced parliament to pass the act of 1766. This act repealed the duties granted by the Sugar Act two years previous. Instead of the duty of three pence on foreign molasses and syrups, one penny was to be levied on every gallon of molasses imported into the colonies.[1] In the place of the export duties on coffee and pimento, duties were imposed on these commodities when transported from one colony to another.[2] By the act of 1764 cambric and French lawn paid duties when imported into the colonies; now these duties were imposed in England when the commodities were exported thence to the colonies.[3]

The brilliant orator, Charles Townshend, was however determined to pursue the policy of his predecessor, *viz.*, that of raising a revenue from the colonies. In 1767 the celebrated acts were passed imposing duties on glass, paper, painters' colors, red and white lead, and tea imported into the colonies.[4] Great opposition was manifested to these taxes, and it was soon seen that the non-importation agreements were harming the English manufacturers of these products. Acting on these considerations, Lord North in 1770 had all the duties granted in 1767 repealed, except the three pence per pound on tea.[5]

---

our fish, a less quantity of the latter will of course be exported. The obvious effect of which must be the diminishing of the fish trade, not only to the West Indies, but to Europe, fish suitable for both these markets being the produce of the same voyage. If, therefore, one of these markets be shut, the other cannot be supplied. The loss of one is the loss of both, as the fishery must fail with the loss of either." *Speeches of the Governors of Massachusetts*, p. 19; *cf.* the petition of the same date, November 3d, 1764, *ibid.*, p. 22; *cf.* also Minot's *History*, ii, p. 147; Bernard's *Select Letters*, p. 8.

[1] 6 Geo. III., c. 52, section v, excepts syrups and molasses from Dominica.

[2] 6 Geo. III., c. 52.   [3] *Ibid.*, § x.

[4] 7 Geo. III., c. 46; *Parliamentary History*, xvi, pp. 375, 376.

[5] 10 Geo. III., c. 17.

In another important respect also England changed her commercial policy at this time. During the earlier period heavy duties were levied on grain and wheat imported into England, while the importation of salt provisions, such as beef, pork, bacon,[1] and butter[2] was absolutely prohibited. These laws made the West India trade an absolute neces- sity to the colonies. Now however the duties were taken off grain from the colonies,[3] and salted provisions were also al- lowed to be imported thence duty free.[4]

In the machinery and methods of administration, a change can also be noted. To insure the execution of the laws, armed vessels, such as the Gaspée, were used.[5] A vice-ad- miralty court for all the colonies was to be established at Halifax.[6] Then writs of assistance[7] began to be employed in executing the laws. One of Charles Townshend's measures was that the King under the Great Seal should appoint com-

---

[1] 18 Charles II., c. 2.   [2] 30 Charles II., c. 2, § ix.

[3] 6 Geo. III., c. 3; 7 Geo. III., c. 4.

[4] 8 Geo. III., c. 9; 14 Geo. III., c. 9. Burke in 1775 said: "The scarcity which you have felt would have been a desolating famine, if this child of your old age, with a true filial piety, with a Roman charity, had not put the full breast of its youthful exuberance to the mouth of its exhausted parent." *Speeches*, i, p. 284.

[5] Chamberlain, vi. Winsor's *Narrative and Critical History*, p. 23.

[6] Burnaby's *Travels;* Bernard, *Select Letters*, p. 16. In Massachusetts it was feared "that the powers given by the late act to the court of vice-admiralty, insti- tuted over all America, are so expressed as to leave it doubtful, whether goods seized for illicit importation in any one of the colonies may not be removed, in order to trial, to any other colony, where the judge may reside, although at many hundred miles distance from the point of seizure. That if this distinction should be admitted, many persons, however legally their goods may have been imported, must lose their property, merely from an inability of following after it, and making that defence which they might do, if the trial had been in the colony, where the goods were seized." *Speeches*, p. 22.

[7] *Cf.* Tudor's *Otis*, p. 86; Adams, *Works*, x, p. 291; ii, pp. 124, 125 n, also ap- pendix, vii, p. 269; especially *Reports of Cases in the Superior Court of Massa- chusetts*, 1761–1772, by Josiah Quincy, Jr., and *Appendix* of Horace Gray, pp. 51, 57; p. 397, 407, *etc.*; Hutchinson, *History of Massachusetts*, iii, pp. 89–93.

missioners of the customs, who were to reside in the colonies.[1]

Many vital changes were also introduced in the policy of eumeration. In 1764 many articles were added to the list viz., coffee, pimento, cocoa-nuts, whalefins, raw silk, hides and skins,[2] pot and pearl ashes,[3] iron and lumber.[4] But the exportation of iron to Ireland was permitted, while lumber could be sent to Ireland, to the Azores and Madeira, or to any part of Europe South of Cape Finisterre.[5] Permission was also given to ship rice directly to any place in America South of the Carolinas.[6] At the same time the duties on rice, when imported into England, were abolished.[7] In 1766 however, the most important change was introduced. In this and the next year it was provided that even the non-enumerated commodities had to be sent either to England, or Ireland,[8] or to some country South of Finisterre.[9]

The former policy of granting bounties to encourage certain industries in the colonies was continued during this pe-

---

[1] 7 Geo. III, c. 41.

[2] Hides and skins were sent to England in great quantities from the Southern colonies, especially from South Carolina. *Cf. Historical Collections of South Carolina*, ii, pp. 129, 131, 237, 254; Sheffield, p. 100. *The Importance of the British Plantations in America* (London, 1731), pp. 71, 80.

[3] In 1769, 1239 tons of potash were sent from America to Great Britain. Sheffield, p. 105. *Cf. Parliamentary History*, xvi, p. 134.

[4] 4 Geo. III., c. 15, §§ xxvii, xxviii.

[5] 5 Geo. III., c. 45, § xxii.

[6] 4 Geo. III., c. 27, § ii; 5 Geo. III., c. 45, § xix; 11 Geo. III., c. 39.

[7] 7 Geo. III., c. 30; 8 Geo. III., c. 2; 9 Geo. III., c. 4; 12 Geo. III., c. 32.

[8] 7 Geo. III., c. 2.

[9] 6 Geo. III., c. 52, § xxx. "The object of the restraint was to prevent a trade even in these articles with countries which had any manufacturers, lest the colonists should find out that they could buy goods cheaper than in England." *The Economic Interpretation of History*, by J. Thorold Rogers, p. 331.

riod.   Bounties were offered for the importation of flax and hemp,[1] lumber,[2] and raw silk.[3]

Numerous changes were also made during these twenty years in the duties payable in England on colonial products, and in the system of drawbacks.[4]   But these changes followed one another most rapidly, and were, for the most part, designed as palliatives to other acts whose execution it was feared would prove onerous.

The acquisition of Canada furnished the occasion for the passage of certain statutes.   Salt for the fisheries was allowed to be directly imported from any part of Europe to Quebec.[5]   Then, since Canada was the great beaver producing country, the duties on beaver imported into England

---

[1] 4 Geo. III., c. 36.   [2] 5 Geo. III., c. 45;   11 Geo. III., c. 50.

[3] 9 Geo. III., c. 38.   For the history of the attempts to raise silk in the colonies, *cf. The Importance of the British Plantations in America* (London, 1731), pp. 62, 63; Bishop, Vol. i; Sainsbury, *Calendar of State Papers*, 1661–1668, pp. 11, 316; Hening, ii, p. 272; Ramsay's *South Carolina*, ii, p. 221; *Historical Collections of South Carolina*, ii, p. 272; Sheffield, *American Commerce*, p. 43; Gee, *Trade*, pp. 92, 93, 125, 131; Macpherson, iii, p. 52.

[4] 4 Geo. III., c. 11, continued the free importation of lumber.   4 Geo. III., c. 15, § xiii, provided that none of the old subsidy of 1660 could be drawn back on foreign goods from the South of Europe or East Indies, reëxported from England to the colonies; § xiv, except calicoes and muslins; *cf* also § xi.   By 5 Geo. III., c. 29, §§ i, ii, the production of raw silk in the colonies was encourged by lessening of duties.   5 Geo. III., c. 45, § xi, encouraged the production of coffee in the colonies by differential duties.   5 Geo. III., c. 45, § xxiii, gave advantages to colonial bar-iron.   7 Geo. III., c. 30, allowed the importation of sago powder and vermicelli from America free of duty.   By 7 Geo. III, c. 45, § vi, the full drawback on colonial coffee and cocoa, if reëxported from England, was allowed.   Section vii. of same statute provided that china earthen-ware exported from England to the colonies should receive no drawback.   10 Geo. III., c. 17, repealed this.   7 Geo. III., c. 56, § ii, provided that the whole duty may be drawn back on tea exported from England to the colonies.   9 Geo. III., c. 39, provided for the free importation of raw hides and skins from the American colonies, *etc., etc.   Cf.* J. Roebuck, *An Enquiry* (London, 1776), pp. 35, 36.

[5] 4 Geo. III., c. 19, §§ i, ii;   6 Geo. III., c. 42.

were lessened, and at the same time no drawback was to be allowed on beaver reëxported from England.[1]

[Before concluding, some mention must be made of certain parliamentary statutes, by which it was sought to coerce the colonies into obedience by attacking their trade.] In 1774 the port of Boston was closed because "the commerce of his Majesty's subjects cannot be safely carried on there, nor the customs payable to his Majesty duly collected."[2]   In the next year the trade of the colonies was restrained to Great Britain, Ireland, and the British West Indies, and the colonies were prohibited from fishing on the banks of Newfoundland.[3]   At this time, however, the Continental Congress had met, and the colonial era was passing away.

§ 2. *Some General Results of the System.*   In tracing the development of England's commercial policy, the effect of individual statutes was noticed.   It was pointed out, that after the enumeration of rice, South Carolina lost control of the Portuguese markets.   When, however, the stringency of the enumeration was mitigated, South Carolina regained those markets.   It remains, however, to point out some general effects of the acts viewed as a system.

Economically the general results of the trade regulations were important,   Robert Giffen has repeatedly pointed out how difficult it is, even with modern comparatively accurate methods, to obtain reliable results from the use of export and import statistics.   This difficulty is immeasurably enhanced when we have to rely on the meagre figures of a century and a half ago.   For we neither know how these statistics were taken, nor at all how accurate they are; while their inadequacy becomes clearly evident when we consider the large amount of smuggling carried on both in England and the colonies.   One general proposition, however, can be

---

[1] 4 Geo. III., c. 9, § i.   [2] 14 Geo. III., c. 19.

[3] 15 Geo. III., c. 10; 15 Geo. III., c. 18.

formulated from the examination of these statistics, and that
is that the balance of trade between England and the colonies
was unfavorable to the latter.[1] And this was an inherent consequence of the mercantile system, by which England regulated these commercial relations. The colonies were unable
to pay England for her manufactures entirely in raw materials, and the residue was paid in coin obtained from the favorable trade with Spain, Portugal, and the West Indies. All
metal had to be sent to England; it was, as De Foe says,
"snatched up for returns to England in specie."[2]

An important consequence followed from this continuous
drain of specie. The colonies could with difficulty retain
coin, and hence were forced either to fall back on barter, or
to issue paper money. In the Northern colonies the balance of trade was far more unfavorable than in the Southern
colonies, while at the same time the former colonies needed
more money on account of their frequent wars. Thus in
1759 New England exported to England commodities to the
value of £37,802, and imported thence £599,647 worth of
goods. During the same year the corresponding figures for
Virginia and Maryland together were £504,451, and £605,-
882.[3] In accord with this state of affairs we find that Massachusetts was the first colony to issue paper money,[4] while
Virginia issued it only towards the end of the colonial era.[5]

---

[1] *Cf. Parliamentary History*, xvi, pp. 483, 484; Macpherson, *Annals of Commerce*, iii. pp. 317, 339, 351, 365, 385; Chalmers, *Revolt*, ii, p. 6; *New York Colonial Documents*, v, pp. 601, 613, 614, 616, 761; Sheffield, *American Commerce*,
appendix, p. 24.

[2] De Foe, *Trade*, p. 360. "That one principal difficulty, which has ever attended the trade of the colonies, proceeds from the scarcity of money, which scarcity is caused by the balance of trade with Great Britain, which has been continually against the colonies, "*Speeches of the Governors of Massachusetts*, p. 23; *cf.
Collections of the New York Historical Society*, Series i, iv, p. 281, Smith says,
"It drains us of all the silver and gold we can collect."

[3] Macpherson, iii, p. 339.   [4] Walker, *Money*, p. 307.

[5] Walker's *Money*, pp. 324, 325.   Virginia issued paper in 1755.

From the above facts it appears legitimate to infer that an important cause for many sad pages in the financial history of the colonies was not so much the ignorance of our ancestors, as the economic forces set in motion by the colonial system of England.[1]

While, on the one hand, the acts of trade and navigation are partially responsible for many sad passages in the fiscal history of the colonies, on the other hand they conduced to the development of a most important colonial industry. This industry was ship-building, for which the colonies were especially adapted on account of the cheapness of lumber. In developing this natural fitness, the protection afforded to English and colonial shipping by the Navigation Acts was an important factor. As a rule England did not discriminate against colonial and in favor of English ships,[2] although the colonies frequently attempted by legislation to secure advantages for their own shipping.[3]

As a result of this policy ship building and the carrying trade increased rapidly, especially in the New England colonies. Child early noticed this feature of New England. "Of all the American Plantations," he writes, "his Majesty hath none so apt for the building of shipping as New England."[4] In 1631 Winthrop built the first vessel,[5] and half a century

[1] A sentence from a pamphlet of John Dickinson, although exhibiting a curious confusion of cause and effect, will bear out this statement. "It is not pretended," he writes, "that the increase of our importations is solely owing to the emissions of paper money; but it is thought to be a very great cause of that increase." *Political Writings*, i, p. 55 n.

[2] The two exceptions are 25 Charles II, c. 7, *cf.* Beverly's *Virginia*, i, p. 68; the other statute was in force only a short time, 12 Geo. II., c. 30.

[3] Hening, vi, p. 97; Chalmers, *Revolt of the Colonies*, ii, p. 33; Bishop, i, pp. 41–62; *Laws of Massachusetts* (1672–1686), p. 69; *New York Colonial Documents*, iii, p. 579; *Spotswood Letters*, i, p. ix.

[4] Child, *On Trade*, p. 215.

[5] Weeden, p. 123; Bishop, i, p. 38.

later New England ships were sold in England.[1] Massachusetts outstripped all the colonies in this industry, while outside of New England it always remained comparatively unimportant.[2] Thus in 1700 Bellomont said, " I believe one
may venture to say there are more good vessels belonging
to the town of Boston than to all Scotland and Ireland."[3]
So important did this industry become that in 1724 the ship
carpenters of the Thames complained to the King, "that
their trade was hurt and their workman emigrated since so
many vessels were built in New England.[4] Massachusetts
built ships not only for England, but also for European
countries,[5] and for the West Indies.[6]

In 1772 one hundred and eighty-two vessels were built in
the colonies, of which New England built one hundred and
twenty-three, while New York and Pennsylvania built only
fifteen and eighteen respectively.[7] While three-quarters of
the vessels trading in New England belonged to these colonies, three-quarters of the vessels trading to Maryland
and Virginia belonged to merchants resident in England.[8]
Early English writers, referring to the rapid development
of English shipping after the Navigation Act, have called
this act the *Sea Magna Charta*[9] and the *Charta Maritima*.[10]

---

[1] *Hutchinson Papers*, ii, p. 232; *Andros Tracts*, ii. p. 114 (Prince Society Publications).

[2] *New York Colonial Documents*, i, p. 160; Chalmers, *Political Annals*, pp.
434, 437, *Revolt*, ii, pp. 12, 34; Macpherson, iii, pp. 164, 165; Bishop, i, pp. 40,
47; Browne's *Maryland*, p. 183.

[3] *New York Colonial Documents*, iv, p. 790.   [4] Chalmers, *Revolt*, ii, p. 33.

[5] *Proceedings of the Massachusetts Historical Society*, 1860–1862, p. 111.

[6] *Ante*, p. 99.

[7] W. C. Ford, *Report on the Trade of Great Britain and the United States*,
January, 1791 (Washington, 1888), p. 20, *cf.* also Lindsay, *History of Merchant
Shipping*, ii, p. 239 n.   [8] *Ibid.*, *cf.* the table, p. 16.

[9] Sir Francis Brewster, *Essays on Trade and Navigation* (London, 1675), p. 92.

[10] Josiah Child, *On Trade*, preface and p. 112.

American historians have, however, failed to note how all-important England's policy was in developing the ship building industry and the carrying trade of New England.

Politically the commercial regulations were not so important. Up to 1763 only slight political importance attaches to the system, for only in a negative way did it affect the political ideas of the colonists. The colonies were peopled by men of varied race and religion, who had little common consciousness of rights and wrongs and few common political ideals. The centrifugal forces among them were strong. Among centripetal forces, such as a common sovereign and a common system of private law, must be reckoned the fact that their commerce was regulated by a system which, as a rule, was uniform for all the colonies. When the acts of trade worked to their advantage, the colonists reaped common benefits; when they inflicted hardships, the colonists made common complaint.

Moreover, the fact that England was unable to enforce certain of her acts, especially the Molasses Act, caused contempt for parliamentary authority. The continued and, by the very nature of things, the necessary violation of this law lead to a questioning of its sanction. while the open favoritism shown in it towards the West India colonies naturally aroused dissaffection in those of the continent.

The colonial system, as it was administered before 1763, contributed but slightly in bringing about the revolution of 1776. As Mr. Ramsay has said, "if no other grievances had been superadded to what existed in 1763, they would have been soon forgotten, for their pressure was neither great, nor universal.[1] It was only when the fundamental basis of the

---

[1] Ramsay, *The History of the American Revolution*, i, p. 43; *cf.* Burke's *Speeches*, i, p. 202, "American Taxation": "But America bore it from the fundamental act of navigation until 1764. Why? because men do bear the inevitable constitution of their original nature with all its infirmities. The act of navigation

acts was changed from one of commercial monopoly to one
of revenue, that the acts became of vital political importance.

attended the colonies from their infancy, grew with their growth, and strengthened
with their strength. They were confirmed in obedience to it, even more by usage
than by law. They scarcely had remembered a time when they were not subject
to such a restraint." For the opposite view *vide* Weeden, *Social and Economic
History*, p. 234; E. G. Scott, *Constitutional Liberty*, p. 198; J. Adams, *Works*,
x, p. 320; R. G. Thwaites, *The Colonies*, p. 106.

BIBLIOGRAPHY.

ADAMS, JOHN. *The Works of.* Edited by Charles Francis Adams. Boston, 1856.

An Additional Act. London, 1657.

ANDERSON, ADAM. *Historical and Chronological Deduction of the Origin of Commerce.* 6 vols. Dublin, 1790.

Andros Tracts, The. In the Prince Society Publications, edited by W. H. Whitmore. 3 vols. Boston, 1868–1874.

ARBER, EDWARD. *English Reprints,* vol. x., containing *A Counterblaste to Tobacco,* by James VI. of Scotland, I. of England. London, 1870.

ASHLEY, JOHN. *Memoirs and Considerations Concerning the Trade and Revenues of the British Colonies in America.* London, 1740.

—— *The Second Part* of above. London, 1743.

—— *A Supplement* to the two other works. London, 1744.

ASHLEY, W. J. *Introduction to English Economic History and Theory.* Part I. London, 1888.

—— *The Early History of the English Woollen Industry,* in Vol. II., No. 4, of the Publications of the American Economic Association.

BACON, SIR FRANCIS. *The Works of.* Collected and Edited by James Spedding, Robert Leslie Ellis, Douglas Denon Heath. Cambridge, 1863.

BAIRD, C. W. *History of the Huguenot Emigration to America.* 2 vols. New York, 1885.

BANCROFT, G. *History of the United States.* Centenary Edition. 6 vols. Boston, 1876–78.

BAUDRILLART, H. *J. Bodin et son Temps.* Paris, 1853.

BELKNAP, JEREMY. *History of New Hampshire.* 2nd Ed. Boston, 1813.

BERNARD, GOVERNOR. *Select Letters on the Trade and Government of America.* London, 1774.

BEVERLEY, R. *The History and Present State of Virginia.* London, 1705.

BIDDLE. *A Memoir of Sebastian Cabot.* London, 1832.

BISHOP, J. LEANDER. *History of American Manufactures.* 3 vols. Philadelphia and London, 1866.

457]   [159

BLAND, RICHARD, of Virginia. *An Enquiry into the Rights of the British Colonies.* London, 1769.

BLANQUI, JÉRÔME–ADOLPHE. *History of Political Economy in Europe.* Translated by Emily J. Leonard. New York and London, 1880.

BODINUS. *De Republica Libri Sex.* Francofurti, 1541.

BOLLES, ALBERT SIDNEY. *Industrial History of the United States.* Norwich, Conn., 1878.

BOZMAN, J. LEEDS. *History of Maryland from 1633–1660.* 2 vols. Baltimore, 1837.

BREWER, J. SHERMAN. *Calendar of Letters and Papers, foreign and domestic, of the reign of Henry VIII.* 4 vols. 1862–1886.

Britannia Languens, or a Discourse of Trade. London, 1680.

BREWSTER, SIR FRANCIS. *Essays on Trade and Navigation.* London, 1695.

BROCK, R. A. In 10th U. S. Census, volume "Reports on the Productions of Agriculture," *A Succinct Account of Tobacco in Virginia.* Washington, 1883.

BRODHEAD, J. ROMEYN. *History of the State of New York.* 2 vols. New York, 1859–1871.

BROWNE, WILLIAM HAND. *Maryland, the History of a Palatinate.* Boston, 1884.

BROUGHAM, H. *Inquiry into the Colonial Policy of the European Powers.* 2 vols. Edinburgh, 1803.

BRUNIALTI, ATTILIO. *Lo Stato Moderno.* Turin, 1891.

BURGESS, JOHN W. *Political Science and Comparative Constitutional Law.* 2 vols. Boston and London, 1891.

BURNABY, REV. ANDREW. *Travels through the Middle Settlements in North America.* London, 1775.

BURKE, EDMUND. *Speeches in the House of Commons and in Westminster-hall.* 4 vols. London, 1816.

CAMPBELL, JOHN LORD. *Lives of the Lord Chancellors.* 4th Ed. 10 vols. London, 1856.

CAMPBELL, J. *Candid and Impartial Considerations on the Nature of the Sugar Trade.* London, 1763.

CARY, JOHN. *A Discourse on Trade and Other Matters Relative to it.* London, 1745.

Case (the) of the Planters of Tobacco, in Virginia. London, 1733.

CHALMERS, G. *Introduction to the History of the Revolt of the American Colonies.* 2 vols. Boston, 1845.

———— *Political Annals of the Present United Colonies.* London, 1780.

────── *Opinions of Eminent Lawyers.* London, 1814.

CHAMBERLAIN, MELLEN. *The Revolution Impending,* in Winsor's "Narrative and Critical History of America," Vol. VI. Boston and New York, 1888.

CHERBURY, EDWARD LORD HERBERT OF. *The Autobiography of.* Edited by Sidney L. Lee. London, 1886.

CHILD, SIR JOSIAH. *A New Discourse of Trade.* 2nd Ed. London, 1694.

COBBETT. *Parliamentary History of England.* London, 1806.

COKE, ROGER. *On Trade,* containing *A Treatise Wherein is demonstrated That the Church and State Of England are in Equal Danger With the Trade Of it and Reasons of the Increase of the Dutch Trade.* London, 1671.

Considerations on the Present State of our Northern Colonies. London, 1763.

COOKE, JOHN ESTEN. *Virginia, a History of the People.* Boston, 1887.

CUNNINGHAM, W. *The Growth of English Industry and Commerce During the Early and Middle Ages.* Cambridge, 1890.

────── *The Growth of English Industry and Commerce in Modern Times.* Cambridge, 1892.

D'AVENANT, CHARLES. *The Political and Commercial Works of that Celebrated Writer.* Collected and revised by Sir Charles Whitworth. 5 vols. London, 1771.

D'EWES, SIR SIMONDS. *The Journals of all the Parliaments during the Reign of Queen Elizabeth.* London, 1682.

DE FOE, DANIEL. *A Plan of the English Commerce.* 3rd Ed. London, 1749.

DICKINSON, JOHN. *The Political Writings of.* 2 vols. Wilmington, 1801.

DINWIDDIE, ROBERT. *The Official Records of.* Edited by R. A. Brock. 2 vols. in the Virginia Historical Society Collections. Richmond, Va., 1883.

Discourse of Trade, Coyn and Paper Credit. London, 1697.

DOWELL, STEPHEN. *History of Taxation and Taxes in England.* 4 vols. London, 1884.

DOYLE, J. ANDREW. *English Colonies in America, Virginia, Maryland and the Carolinas.* New York, 1882.

────── *English in America, the Puritan Colonies.* 2 vols. London, 1887.

DRAYTON, JOHN. *View of South Carolina.* Charleston, 1802.

Edinburgh Review. Vol. 51, pp. 419–427. "Rise, Progress, and Decline of Commerce in Holland."

EDWARDS, BRYAN. *The History, Civil and Commercial of the British Colonies in the West Indies.* 2 vols. London, 1793.

ELLIOTT, ORRIN LESLIE. *The Tariff Controversy,* in Leland Stanford Junior University Monographs, History and Economics, No. I. Palo Alto, 1892.

England, The Statutes at large of.

FABER, DR. RICHARD. *Die Entstehung des Agrarschutzes in England.* Strassburg, 1888.

FISHER, E. T. *Report of a French Protestant Refugee in Boston in 1687,* in Shea's " Early Southern Facts," No. I. Brooklyn, 1868.

FISHER, GEORGE PARK. *The Colonial Era.* New York, 1892.

FORCE, PETER. *Tracts and other Papers.* 4 vols. Washington, 1836–46.

FORD, PAUL LEICESTER. *List of Some Briefs in Appeal Causes.* Brooklyn, 1889.

FORD, W. C. *Report on the Trade of Great Britain with the United States, January, 1791.* Washington, 1888.

FORSTER, SAMUEL. *A Digest of all the Laws.* London, 1727.

FORTREY, SAMUEL. *England's Interest and Improvement.* Cambridge, 1663. London, 1673.

FORSYTH, WILLIAM. *Cases and Opinions on Constitutional Law.* London, 1879.

FRANKLIN, BENJAMIN. *The Works of.* Edited by Jared Sparks. Boston, 1840.

FRENCH, B. F. *History of the Rise and Progress of the Iron Trade of the United States.* N. Y., 1858.

FROTHINGHAM, RICHARD. *The Rise of the Republic of the United States.* Boston, 1886.

GARDINER, SAMUEL RAWSON. *Prince Charles and the Spanish Marriage.* 2 vols. London, 1869.

GEE, JOSHUA. *Trade and Navigation of Great Britain Considered.* 3d. ed. London, 1731.

GREEN, J. R. *History of the English People.* 4 vols. New York, 1880.

GREY, see Quincy.

GROSS, CHARLES. *Gild Merchant.* 2 vols. Oxford, 1890.

HAKLUYT, RICHARD. *The Third and Last Volume of the Voyages, Navigations, Traffiques, and Discoveries of the English Nation.* London, 1600.

HALL, HUBERT. *History of the Custom-Revenue in England.* 2 vols. London, 1885.

HARDY, THOMAS DUFFUS. *Syllabus of the Documents in Rymer's Foldera.* 3 vols. London, 1869–85.

HAWKS, FRANCIS L. *History of North Carolina.* Fayetteville, N. C., 1857.

HAZARD, EBENEZER. *Historical Collections consisting of State Papers.* Vol. I. Philadelphia, 1792.

HEWAT, (HEWIT, HEWATT). *An Historical Account, of the Rise and Progress of the Colonies of South Carolina and Georgia.* London, 1779.

HOLMES, A. *The Annals of America, from the Discovery by Columbus in the year 1492 to the year 1826.* 2nd ed. 2 vols. Cambridge, 1829.

HOSMER, JAMES R. *A Short History of Anglo-Saxon Freedom.* N. Y., 1890.

———— *Samuel Adams.* Boston and New York, 1889.

HOWARD, GEORGE E. *An Introduction to the Local Constitutional History of the United States.* Baltimore, 1889.

HUME, DAVID. *The History of England.* 6 vols. N. Y., 1879.

HUSKISSON, THE RIGHT HON. W. *Speech on the Navigation Laws.* London, 1826.

HUTCHINSON, THOMAS. *History of Massachusetts.* 3 vols. Vols. I. and II. Boston, 1795; Vol. III. London, 1824.

Hutchinson Papers. 2 vols. Prince Society Publications. Albany, 1865.

Importance [the] of the British Plantations in America to this Kingdom. London, 1731.

JAMES I. OF ENGLAND, see Arber.

JEFFERSON, THOMAS. *Notes on the State of Virginia.* London, 1787.

JOHNSON, CAPT. EDWARD. *Wonder-Working Providence of Sions Saviour in New England.* Edited by W. F. Poole. Andover, 1867.

LECKY, W. E. H. *A History of England in the Eighteenth Century.* N. Y., 1888.

———— *The Political Value of History.* N. Y., 1893.

LEROY-BEAULIEU, PAUL. *De la Colonisation chez les peuples modernes.* 3rd ed. Paris, 1886.

LINDSAY, W. SHAW. *History of Merchant Shipping and Ancient Commerce.* 4 vols. London, 1874.

Letter (A) to a Member of Parliament concerning the Naval Store-Bill. London, 1720.

LODGE, HENRY CABOT. *A Short History of the English Colonies in America* New York, 1881.

LONG. *The History of Jamaica.* 3 vols. London, 1784.

LONGMAN, WILLIAM. *The History of the Life and Times of Edward the Third.* 2 vols. London, 1869.

LOW, SIDNEY J., and PULLING, F. S. *Dictionary of English History.* 2nd Ed. London, Paris, New York and Melbourne, 1885.

MACAULAY, THOMAS BABINGTON. *The History of England from the Accession of James* 5 vols. Phil.

MACPHERSON, DAVID. *Annals of Commerce, Manufactures, Fisheries, and Navigation.* 4 vols. London, 1805.

M'CULLOCH, J. R. *A Dictionary of Commerce and Commercial Navigation.* London, 1869.

Massachusetts Bay, Records of the Government and Company of the.

Massachusetts, Colonial Laws of, 1672–1686. Ed. William H. Whitmore. Boston, 1887.

Massachusetts, Colonial Laws of, 1660–1672. Ed. William H. Whitmore. Boston, 1889.

Massachusetts Historical Society, Collections of the.

Massachusetts Historical Society, Proceedings of the.

Memorials presented by the Deputies of the Council of Trade in France to the Royal Council in 1701. London, 1737.

MERIVALE, HERMAN. *Lectures on Colonization and Colonies.* 2 vols. London, 1841.

MINOT, G. RICHARDS. *Continuation of the History of the Province of Massachusetts Bay.* 2 vols. Boston, 1798, 1803.

MITCHELL, J. (M. D.). *The Present State of Great Britain and North America.* London, 1767.

MONT, J. M. *Corps Universel Diplomatique.* Amsterdam, 1728.

MORLEY, JOHN. *Walpole.* London and New York, 1889.

NEILL, REV. E. DUFFIELD. *Virginia Carolorum.* Albany, 1886.

——— *History of the Virginia Company of London.* Albany, 1869.

New York Historical Society, Collections of the.

New York, Documents Relating to the Colonial History of the State of New York. 13 vols. Edited by Brodhead and O'Callaghan. Albany, 1856–81.

North Carolina, The Colonial Records of. Edited by Saunders.

O'CALLAGHAN, EDMUND BURKE. *Documentary History of the State of New York.* Ed. 1850.

——— *History of New Netherland.* New York, 1846.

OCHENKOWSKI, W. VON. *Englands wirthschaftliche Entwickelung im Ausgange des Mittelalters.* Jena, 1879.

OSGOOD, H. L. *England and the Colonies.* Political Science Quarterly, II, p. 440.

OVIEDO Y VALDÉS, GONZALO FERNANDEZ DE. *La Hystoria general de las Indias.* Salamanca, 1547.

PALFREY, J. GORHAM. *History of New England.* 5 vols. Boston, 1859–90.

PARKMAN, FRANCIS. *Old Régime in Canada.* Boston, 1874.

PEDLEY, CHARLES. *The History of Newfoundland.* London, 1863.

POSTLETHWAYT, MALACHY. *Great Britain's True System.* London, 1757.

—— *Britain's Commercial Interest Explained and Improved.* 2 vols. London, 1757.

—— *The Importance of the African Expedition.* London, 1758.

—— *Universal Dictionary of Trade and Commerce*, by *Savary.* 2d. ed. 2 vols. London, 1757.

POWNALL, THOMAS. *Administration of the Colonies.* 2d ed. London, 1765,

Present State (the) of the British and French Trade to Africa and America. London, 1745.

PRESTON, HOWARD W. *Documents Illustrative of American History, 1606–1860.* New York and London, 1886.

PRINGSHEIM, OTTO. *Beiträge zur Wirtschaftlichen Entwickelungsgeschichte der Vereinigten Niederlande im 17 und 18 Jahrhundert.* No. III. of vol. X. of Schmoller's *Forschungen.*

QUINCY, JOSIAH. *Reports of Cases argued and adjudged, 1761–1772.* Ed. by S. M. Quincy, with an appendix on the Writs of Assistance by Grey. Boston, 1865.

RALEIGH, SIR WALTER. *Works.* Ed. by Birch. 2 vols. London, 1751.

RAMSAY, D. *History of South Carolina.* 2 vols. Charleston, 1807.

—— *History of the American Revolution.* 2 vols. Philadelphia, 1789.

RANKE, LEOPOLD V. *A History of England, principally in the seventeenth century.* Oxford, 1875.

RAYNAL, GUILLAUME THOMAS. *Histoire Philosophique et Politique des Établissemens et du Commerce des Europeéns dans les deux Indes.* 12 vols. Paris, 1820.

REEVES, JOHN. *History of the Law of Shipping and Navigation.* Dublin, 1792.

REYNELL, CAREW. *The True English Interest* (1674). In Sir Charles Whitworth's *Scarce Tracts on Trade and Commerce.* 2 vols. London, 1777.

RHODE ISLAND COLONIAL RECORDS.

RIPLEY, WILLIAM ZEBINA. *The Financial History of Virginia.* Vol. IV. no. 1, of Columbia College Studies in History, Economics and Public Law. New York, 1893.

ROEBUCK, J. *Enquiry Whether the Guilt of the Present Civil War in America Ought to be Imputed to Great Britain or America.* London, 1776.

ROBERTS, ELLIS H. *New York.* 2 vols. Boston and New York, 1890.

ROGERS, JAMES E. THOROLD. *The Economic Interpretation of History.* New York, 1888.

ROSCHER, W. *Kolonien, Kolonialpolitik und Auswanderung.* 2nd ed. Leipzig, 1856.

RYMER, THOMAS. *Fœdera, Conventiones, Literæ.* 20 vols. London, 1726–35.

SAINSBURY, W. NOEL. *Calendar of State Papers, Colonial Series.* London, 1860–1884.

SAXBY, H. *British Customs.* London, 1757.

SCHANZ, G. *Englische Handelspolitik gegen Ende des Mittelalters.* 2 vols. Leipzig, 1881.

SCHARF, J. F. *History of Maryland.* 2 vols. Baltimore, 1879.

SCHOMBURGK, SIR ROBERT H. *The History of Barbados.* London, 1848.

SCHUYLER, G. W. *Colonial New York.* 2 vols. New York., 1885.

SCOBELL. *Collection of Acts and Ordinances of General Use.* 2 vols. London, 1658.

Scotland, The Acts of Parliaments of. 1820.

SCOTT, EBEN GREENOUGH. *The Development of Constitutional Liberty in the English Colonies of America.* New York, 1882.

SCRIVENOR, HARRY. *History of the Iron Trade.* London, 1854,

SEELEY, J. R. *The Expansion of England.* London, 1888.

SHEFFIELD, 'JOHN BAKER. *Observations on the Commerce of the American States.* London, 1784.

SPARKS, JARED. *The Diplomatic Correspondence of the American Revolution.*

SMITH, ADAM. *An Inquiry into the Nature and Causes of the Wealth of Nations.* Ed. by J. E. Th. Rogers. 2 vols. Oxford, 1880.

SMITH, CAPTAIN JOHN. *The True Travels, Adventures and Observations.* 2 vols. Richmond, 1819, from London, 1629.

Speeches of the Governors of Massachusetts from 1765–1775; and The Answers of the House of Representatives to the Same. Boston, 1818.

SPOTSWOOD, GOVERNOR. *The Letters of.* Virginia Historical Society Publications.

STANHOPE, EARL. *Life of William Pitt.* 4 vols. London, 1861.

STEBBING, WILLIAM. *Sir Walter Ralegh.* Oxford, 1891.

STILLÉ, C. J. *Life and Times of John Dickinson.* Philadelphia, 1891.

STITH, WILLIAM. *The History of Virginia.* London, 1753.

STUBBS, WILLIAM. *The Constitutional History of England.* 3 vols. Oxford, 1883–84.

SWANK, JAMES M. *History of the Manufacture of Iron in all Ages.* Philadelphia, 1884.

THURLOE, JOHN. *A Collection of the State Papers of.* 7 vols. London, 1742.

THWAITES, REUBEN GOLD. *The Colonies, 1492–1750.* New York and London, 1893.

TOWNSHEND, CHARLES. *Remarks on the Letter Address'd to Two Great Men in a Letter to the Author of that Piece.* London, 1760.

TUCKER. *Cui Bono?* Gloucester, 1781.

TUDOR, W. *Life of James Otis of Mass.* Boston, 1893.

WALKER, FRANCIS A. *Money.* New York, 1891.

WASHBURN, EMORY. *Sketches of the Judicial History of Massachusetts.* Boston, 1840.

WEEDEN, WILLIAM BABCOCK. *Economic and Social History of New England, 1620–1789.* 2 vols. Boston, 1890.

WHITLOCKE. *Memorials of the English Affairs.* London, 1682.

WICQUEFORT, DE. *L'Histoire des Provinces-Unies.* 1743.

WINTHROP, JOHN. *The History of New England.* Ed. by James Savage. 2 vols. Boston, 1825–26.

WITT, JAN DE. *True Interest and Political Maxims of the Republic of Holland.* London, 1746.

WOOD, WILLIAM. *A Survey of Trade.* London, 1718.

YOUNG, ARTHUR. *A Tour in Ireland.* 2 vols. Dublin, 1780.